At Issue

RFID Technology

Other Books in the At Issue Series:

At Issue

RFID Technology

Roman Espejo

GREENHAVEN PRESS
A part of Gale, Cengage Learning

GALE
CENGAGE Learning·

Detroit • New York • San Francisco • New Haven, Conn • Waterville, Maine • London

GALE
CENGAGE Learning™

Christine Nasso, *Publisher*
Elizabeth Des Chenes, *Managing Editor*

For more information, contact:
Greenhaven Press
27500 Drake Rd.
Farmington Hills, MI 48331-3535
Or you can visit our Internet site at gale.cengage.com

Articles in Greenhaven Press anthologies are often edited for length to meet page requirements. In addition, original titles of these works are changed to clearly present the main thesis and to explicitly indicate the author's opinion. Every effort is made to ensure that Greenhaven Press accurately reflects the original intent of the authors. Every effort has been made to trace the owners of copyrighted material.

Cover image © Images.com/Corbis.

LIBRARY OF CONGRESS CATALOGING-IN-PUBLICATION DATA

RFID technology / Roman Espejo, book editor.
    p. cm. -- (At issue)
Includes bibliographical references and index.
ISBN 978-0-7377-4296-1 (hardcover)
ISBN 978-0-7377-4295-4 (pbk.)
1. Radio frequency identification systems. 2. Privacy, Right of. I. Espejo, Roman, 1977-.
  TK6570.I34.R487 2009
  323.44'8--dc22

        2008045080

Contents

Introduction

In April 2004, the Baja Beach Club in Barcelona, Spain, became known for something other than its swimsuit-sporting waitresses and bare-chested bartenders—it became the first nightclub in the world to offer its patrons radio-frequency identification (RFID) implants, which contain identifying and other personal data that can be scanned with an RFID reader. Linked to a computerized ID and debit system, the implants allow clubgoers to breeze through entry and settle bar tabs with a swipe over their upper arms, the designated location of the rice-sized microchips. "One of our owners wanted to do something special for our new VIP section," states Steve van Soest, the nightclub's spokesperson. About thirty or so Baja Beach Club members are said to have gone through the procedure, which is performed by resident medical staff.

That fall, CNN reporter Robyn Curnow got "chipped" and joined the Baja VIP Club. All it took was a momentary jab into her anesthetized skin with a syringe, but at the time of removal, several complications arose. The RFID implant had migrated about a centimeter from the original site of implantation; even an X-ray did not help doctors precisely determine its location in Curnow's arm. As a result, the adventurous reporter required surgery to be "unchipped" (with the aid of a sophisticated sensor and two monitors), leaving an eight-millimeter scar that she believes "was probably too high a price to pay for becoming a member of the Baja Beach Club."

In the United States, human RFID implants were approved by the Food and Drug Administration in late 2004 as well. But unlike the Baja Beach Club, which uses human RFID tags to up the ante of exclusivity, early adopters in this country have made headlines in different ways. For example, Amal Graafstra, an entrepreneur in Bellingham, Washington, has one RFID implant in each hand that he uses to log onto his computer, open his front door, and start his car and motorcycle. Graafstra was inspired to get implants after managing servers at a medical facility, which required him to carry keys to almost a hundred doors and drawers. "It struck me that modern keys are just crude identification devices, little changed in centuries," he explains. "Even if each lock were unique—most aren't—keys can be copied in any hardware store and, once distributed, are hard to control." Graafstra underwent the procedure in 2005, and his girlfriend followed suit. A year later, surveillance company CityWatcher.com, based in Cincinnati, Ohio, had several employees implanted with RFID chips in their biceps in an attempt to heighten the security of the company's data center.

These examples of RFID human implantation have given rise to a number of ethical and medical questions. In reaction to the CityWatcher.com case, Katherine Albrecht, coauthor of *Spy Chips: How Major Corporations and Government Plan to Track Your Every Move*, argues, "It's wrong to link a person's paycheck with getting an implant. Once people begin 'voluntarily' getting chipped to perform their job duties, it won't be long before pressure gets applied to those who refuse." Her opposition of RFID also espouses the objections some Christians may have to the implants: "When I was eight years old, my grandmother sat me down after a visit to a grocery store and told me that there will be a time when people will not be able to buy or sell food without a number, referring to the Mark of the Beast, Revelations XIII [chapter in Bible]," Albrecht said in 2003. Three years later, she explained, "My goal as a Christian [is] to sound the alarm."

In addition, some researchers suggest that, beyond complicated unchippings such as Robyn Curnow's, RFID implants may pose a serious health risk. For example, retired toxicologist Keith Johnson performed studies in the mid-1990s in which he linked the implants to cancerous growths in lab rats and mice. As for their security, numerous technology experts allege that data stored in human RFID implants can be surreptitiously read and reproduced by hackers for the purpose of identity theft. At a 2006 conference in New York City, one presenter demonstrated that a crude antenna and laptop could capture the signal—and the unique code—emitted by his copresenter's implant.

Proponents of RFID technology hit back at these claims. In response to Albrecht's statements, Mark Roberti, founder of *RFID Journal*, declares that "her views raise the question of whether she is hyping privacy concerns to achieve her religious goals." Roberti also maintains that religious arguments against technology should not have a place in public policy, "The press and policy makers need to separate religious-driven opposition to RFID from questions about how RFID should be used and how individual privacy should be protected."

Some members of the technology community are equally skeptical of RFID's supposed cancer link. For instance, Kevin Warwick, cybernetics professor and one-time RFID implantee, asserts, "[I]n practice, many animals have had such implants in place for several years now (quite a few humans, too), and I have not heard of one single case of there being a problem." Similarly, others have less urgent views of the security of the data in RFID implants. Speaking about the possibility of the implants as carriers of medical records, research scientist Ben Adida suggests, "It's unlikely someone would want to falsify your identity for medical treatment, but likely they would try to intercept your credentials if monetary gain was possible."

The RFID stories of the Baja Beach Club, Amal Graafstra, and CityWatcher.com have helped to put RFID implants on the media's radar because of their futuristic edge. But the adoption of the technology in supply chains, stores, libraries, toll booths, and other places have been steadily trickling into everyday life, making it into pockets, purses, and shopping bags with less fanfare. In *At Issue: RFID Technology*, the authors investigate the impact of this technology.

1

RFID Technology Is Growing

Nancy Friedrich

Nancy Friedrich is editor of Microwaves & RF, *a magazine for radio-frequency engineers.*

A radio-frequency identification (RFID) tag is a miniature chip that stores an identification number that is transmitted by a built-in antenna to an RFID reader. New applications and capabilities of this low-cost, easy-to-use, disposable tag are emerging rapidly, expanding beyond the management of the global supply chain. For instance, RFID's ability to transmit shipment data, such as location and condition, in real time can be employed by the military and government to increase the security of ports. "Smart labels" embedded with anticounterfeiting RFID tags that break apart when tampered with are another recent development. And cell phones and handheld devices equipped with RFID readers will perform a wide variety of tasks, including reading RFID medical tags that instantly detect and warn of harmful drug interactions. From the military to merchandising, RFID is proving to be a versatile, innovative, and reliable technology.

Radio-frequency identification (RFID) is widely used to identify and track objects, animals, or people. Its applications range from tagging retail goods and inventory control to enabling payment, providing secure identification, and tracking animals. Much of the popularity of RFID tags stems from

Nancy Friedrich, "RFID Innovations Deepen Market Penetration," *Microwaves & RF*, July 2007. http://mwrf.com. Copyright © 2007 Penton Media, Inc. All rights reserved. Reproduced by permission.

the fact that they are low in cost, disposable, and easy to use. Essentially, each tag houses a miniature chip transmitter that stores an identification number. An antenna allows the chip to transmit that ID number to a reader. As long as the reader uses the right RF signal, it can read the information from the tag. These characteristics are not fixed, however, and RFID is still evolving. Thanks to ongoing development and innovation, the technology will add capabilities and expand its reach.

An example of such an innovation is a new active RFID platform. Although RFID usually offers minimal security, this platform plans to serve high-value assets. It hails from Hi-G-Tek (North Bethesda, MD). Rather than just detect where an asset is, the company's technology also checks its status or condition in real time. The platform relies on full two-way active RFID communication with miniaturized battery-operated electronic tags, seals, and locks. Using these components, readers can reliably control objects while covering areas of a few hundred meters. Aside from collecting data, the readers are monitored from remote centers in severe environments and over long time periods.

At the heart of this active RFID platform is a chip set, which integrates the device's monitoring functions and the low-frequency circuitry used for close-range communication. These aspects operate seamlessly with the long-range, high-frequency communication channel. In addition, an antenna is integrated in both the printed-circuit board (PCB) and the chip set without any loss in efficiency. To optimize the integrated circuit's (IC's) capabilities, microcontroller software algorithms, communication protocols, and scheduling are employed. They promise to keep the PCB component count and power consumption to a minimum.

Increasing Government and Military Use

While this platform seeks to make RFID suitable for high-value assets, another product suite plans to speed the development of turnkey supply-chain solutions. This product family comes from the Savi Group, which was formed [in November 2006] by Lockheed Martin (Bethesda, MD). Aside from commercial customers, the company plans to serve the U.S. Department of Homeland Security, U.S. Department of Defense (including the U.S. Transportation Command and Defense Logistics Agency), and port and terminal operators.

Essentially, Savi provides integrated real-time information solutions and services for securing and managing global supply chains. The Savi Group aligns Lockheed Martin's decision-support system expertise for large government In-Transit Visibility (ITV), cargo security, and asset-management efforts with Savi Technology's real-time, RFID-based data collection and management capabilities for supply chains. Savi Networks provides information services, which are based on wireless data transmissions, on the location, security, and condition of cargo shipments as they are transported end-to-end throughout the global supply chain. Such products could obviously help the U.S. strengthen its port security measures. In fact, one of the company's initial charters will be to leverage the existing Savi Networks joint venture between Savi Technology and Hutchison Port Holdings, the world's largest port operator.

The company's data-collection level of tags, readers, and signposts are all built on its EchoPoint technology. By employing a unique multi-frequency design and three-element system architecture, this technology achieves both reliable long-range communication and short-range locating capability. Savi's suite of active RFID tags includes general asset tags, which have a smaller form factor and a lower price point for the real-time tracking of supply-chain assets. In addition, the high-performance data-rich tags can store up to 128 kB of data. They are designed to last the life of the asset. Finally, Savi's SensorTags were designed to secure and monitor the integrity and condition of containers and their contents. The company's fixed RFID devices, the Savi Fixed Reader and Savi Signposts, collect data at fixed locations throughout the supply chain. The company also offers Mobile RFID Systems. These mobile devices collect data in an online or offline store-and-forward mode. A variety of software solutions round out these offerings.

Growth in Retail Applications

Government agencies and the military are certainly increasing their use of RFID technologies. Ever since Wal-Mart committed to using RFID, however, the technology also has experienced steady growth in retail applications. Here, RFID is generally used in the tagging of apparel, books, pallets, and cases. Through a joint RFID applications development program, Hyan Microelectronics Co. Ltd. (Shenzhen, China) and Parelec, Inc. (Rocky Hill, NJ) developed an anti-counterfeiting smart label. This label affixes inside or outside a product package. The breakable paper-base tag is printed with a silver antenna. The 30 [to] 35-mm label is designed to break instantly if someone tries to remove it, thereby demonstrating a product's authenticity. . . .

In addition, the two companies developed RFID-based transit tickets with crease-proof antennas. Thanks to a unique manufacturing process, the antennas will continue to function despite being pulled and bent. Last month, Parelec also made news with its acquisition of Precision Systems (Raanana, Israel). Parelec's expertise in mid-range, passive RFID tag technology will now be coupled with Precision Systems' expertise in active RFID and real-time location systems. The companies hope to eventually enable the tracking of products from item level to end use.

Typically, RFID tags are one-time use only. Yet many individuals in the retail sector are recognizing a need to track assets as they move through the supply chain. The Kennedy Group's RFID group (Willoughby, OH), for example, has expanded its line of reusable RFID products. The SmartCard, SmartCard Plus, and SmartCard Premium can now be embedded in or clipped onto reusable transport packaging (containers, racks, and pallets) to track assets as they move through the supply chain. To reduce overall cost, the cards can be programmed and used multiple times. The SmartCards operate in the ultra-high-frequency (915 MHz) and high-frequency (13.56 MHz) RFID spectrums. Despite the great number of RFID products already on the market, a large number of new developments are in the works. For example, Mems-ID Pty Ltd. (Melbourne, Australia) is developing a tracking solution that targets the logistics and safety requirements in the medical devices market. The company's technology is based on a microelectromechanical-systems (MEMS) chip that is mechanical rather than electronic. As such, it promises to provide significant advantages over current electronic RFID chips. For instance, Mems-ID chips can be placed directly onto medical devices, such as surgical instruments. They also can withstand high-temperature autoclave and irradiation sterilization processes.

[In 2006], Mems-ID completed a proof-of-concept chip and reader system. It is currently working toward a beta chip and interrogator algorithm. Initially, the company is focused on developing its technology to track surgical instruments. It expects to undertake a trial with a major orthopedic device company by the middle of [2007].

Clearly, RFID is already a technology success story.

Cell Phones and Handheld Devices

RFID developments are even targeting cell phones and other handheld devices. [In June 2007], Gentag, Inc. (Washington, DC) announced the issuance of Patent 7,148,803, which is entitled, "Radio Frequency Identification (RFID) Based Sensor

Networks." This patent is actually co-owned between Altivera, LLC—a Gentag-operated company—and Symbol Technologies (Motorola). Gentag and Symbol each have independent assignment rights. The broad patent covers the uses of personal wireless devices like cell phones, personal digital assistants (PDAs), and laptops as low-cost wireless readers for RFID sensors. It also covers the creation of RFID-sensor networks for consumer, industrial, and government applications. The patent provides the basis for the creation of a next-generation wireless technology that will put low-cost wireless readers in the hands of consumers, wireless networks, geolocation, and disposable wireless sensors for various market applications. The emergence of nearfield communications (NFC) is expected to accelerate the availability of RFID cell phones.

RFID-reader-enabled cell phones are either currently available or under development with major cell-phone manufacturers worldwide for both the 13.56 MHz and ultra-high (Gen-2) frequencies. In the future, some market forecasts predict that up to one out of two phones will be RFID-reader enabled. By combining RFID cell phones and RFID sensors with cellular networks or the Internet, the consumer will be able to read any RFID sensor tag for almost any application. Examples include using an RFID cell phone to ensure that a drug interaction is unlikely to occur before taking a given medication. Gentag is especially focused on combining RFID cell phones with RFID sensors for specialized diagnostic applications. Under existing Gentag patents, RFID sensors can be integrated into low-cost disposable diagnostic devices like "smart" disposable wireless skin patches or personal drug-delivery systems. They can then be read directly with a cell phone.

These examples offer just a small sampling of the many emerging developments and applications for RFID technology. Keep in mind that RFID's development varies according to different geographic regions. Some countries are heavily investing in the technology while a few have only lightly adopted it. Still others are using RFID for applications that many had not even thought suitable. Clearly, RFID is already a technology success story. It has become entrenched in many sectors ranging from retail to military. Yet it continues to find new applications—just as engineers keep unveiling new RFID capabilities.

2

RFID Technology May Be Vulnerable

Annalee Newitz

Annalee Newitz is a technology and science journalist who has a syndicated weekly column, Techsploitation.

Automatic, cheap, and convenient, radio-frequency identification (RFID) technology is exploding. It is used to start cars and track inventory, and human RFID implants for medical purposes may follow its standard placement in newly issued American passports. Despite its rapid adoption, however, these tags are open to attack. Armed with commercially available equipment, hackers can easily steal, clone, or overwrite the codes in RFID-enabled badges, smart cards, and price chips, breaking into offices, cheating gas pumps, and switching the prices of merchandise. These "digital pickpockets" highlight the most frightening vulnerabilities of RFID—even the tags with the most sophisticated encryption may be cracked or tampered with. This means that the sensitive data in RFID American passports and human implants is not so safe after all.

James Van Bokkelen is about to be robbed. A wealthy software entrepreneur, Van Bokkelen will be the latest victim of some punk with a laptop. But this won't be an email scam or bank account hack. A skinny 23-year-old named Jonathan Westhues plans to use a cheap, homemade USB device to swipe the office key out of Van Bokkelen's back pocket.

Annalee Newitz, "The RFID Hacking Underground," *Wired*, vol. 15, May 2006. http://wired.com. Copyright © 2006 CondNet, Inc. All rights reserved. Reproduced by permission.

"I just need to bump into James and get my hand within a few inches of him," Westhues says. We're shivering in the early spring air outside the offices of Sandstorm, the Internet security company Van Bokkelen runs north of Boston. As Van Bokkelen approaches from the parking lot, Westhues brushes past him. A coil of copper wire flashes briefly in Westhues' palm, then disappears.

Van Bokkelen enters the building, and Westhues returns to me. "Let's see if I've got his keys," he says, meaning the signal from Van Bokkelen's smartcard badge. The card contains an RFID sensor chip, which emits a short burst of radio waves when activated by the reader next to Sandstorm's door. If the signal translates into an authorized ID number, the door unlocks.

Nobody thought about building security features into the Internet in advance, and now we're paying for it in viruses and other attacks. We're likely to see the same thing with RFIDs.

The coil in Westhues' hand is the antenna for the wallet-sized device he calls a cloner, which is currently shoved up his sleeve. The cloner can elicit, record, and mimic signals from smartcard RFID chips. Westhues takes out the device and, using a USB cable, connects it to his laptop and downloads the data from Van Bokkelen's card for processing. Then, satisfied that he has retrieved the code, Westhues switches the cloner from Record mode to Emit. We head to the locked door.

"Want me to let you in?" Westhues asks. I nod.

He waves the cloner's antenna in front of a black box attached to the wall. The single red LED blinks green. The lock clicks. We walk in and find Van Bokkelen waiting.

"See? I just broke into your office!" Westhues says gleefully. "It's so simple." Van Bokkelen, who arranged the robbery "just to see how it works," stares at the antenna in Westhues' hand. He knows that Westhues could have performed his wireless pickpocket maneuver and then returned with the cloner after hours. Westhues could have walked off with tens of thousands of dollars' worth of computer equipment—and possibly source code worth even more. Van Bokkelen mutters, "I always thought this might be a lousy security system."

In Its Early Stages

RFID chips are everywhere—companies and labs use them as access keys, Prius owners use them to start their cars, and retail giants like Wal-Mart have deployed them as inventory tracking devices. Drug manufacturers like Pfizer rely on chips to track pharmaceuticals. The tags are also about to get a lot more personal: Next-gen[eration] U.S. passports and credit cards will contain RFIDs, and the medical industry is exploring the use of implantable chips to manage patients. According to the RFID market analysis firm IDTechEx, the push for digital inventory tracking and personal ID systems will expand the current annual market for RFIDs from $2.7 billion to as much as $26 billion by 2016.

RFID technology dates back to World War II, when the British put radio transponders in Allied aircraft to help early radar system crews detect good guys from bad guys. The first chips were developed in research labs in the 1960s, and by the next decade the U.S. government was using tags to electronically authorize tracks coming into Los Alamos National Laboratory and other secure facilities. Commercialized chips became widely available in the '80s, and RFID tags were being used to track difficult-to-manage property like farm animals and railroad cars. But over the last few years, the market for RFIDs has exploded, driven by advances in computer databases and declining chip prices. Now dozens of companies, from Motorola to Philips to Texas Instruments, manufacture the chips.

The tags work by broadcasting a few bits of information to specialized electronic readers. Most commercial RFID chips are passive emitters, which means they have no onboard battery: They send a signal only when a reader powers them with a squirt of electrons. Once juiced, these chips broadcast their signal indiscriminately within a certain range, usually a few inches to a few feet. Active emitter chips with internal power can send signals hundreds of feet; these are used in the automatic toll-paying devices (with names like FasTrak and E-ZPass) that sit on car dashboards, pinging tollgates as autos whiz through.

For protection, RFID signals can be encrypted. The chips that will go into U.S. passports, for example, will likely be coded to make it difficult for unauthorized readers to retrieve their onboard information (which will include a person's name, age, nationality, and photo). But most commercial RFID tags don't include security, which is expensive: A typical passive RFID chip costs about a quarter, whereas one with encryption capabilities runs about $5. It's just not cost-effective for your average office building to invest in secure chips.

Libramation has sold 5 million RFID tags in a "convenient" unlocked state.

This leaves most RFIDs vulnerable to cloning or—if the chip has a writable memory area, as many do—data tampering. Chips that track product shipments or expensive equipment, for example, often contain pricing and item information. These writable areas can be locked, but often they aren't, because the companies using RFIDs don't know how the chips work or because the data fields need to be updated frequently. Either way, these chips are open to hacking.

"The world of RFID is like the Internet in its early stages," says Ari Juels, research manager at the high tech security firm RSA Labs. "Nobody thought about building security features into the Internet in advance, and now we're paying for it in viruses and other attacks. We're likely to see the same thing with RFIDs."

Purely a Test

David Molnar is a soft-spoken computer science graduate student who studies commercial uses for RFIDs at UC [University of California] Berkeley. I meet him in a quiet branch of the Oakland Public Library, which, like many modern libraries, tracks most of its inventory with RFID tags glued inside the covers of its books. These tags, made by Libramation, contain several writable memory "pages" that store the books' barcodes and loan status.

Brushing a thatch of dark hair out of his eyes, Molnar explains that about a year ago he discovered he could destroy the data on the books' passive-emitting RFID tags by wandering the aisles with an off-the-shelf RFID reader-writer and his laptop. "I would never actually do something like that, of course," Molnar reassures me in a furtive whisper, as a non-bookish security guard watches us.

Our RFID-enabled checkout is indeed quite convenient. As we leave the library, we stop at a desk equipped with a monitor and arrange our selections, one at a time, face up on a metal plate. The titles instantly appear onscreen. We borrow four books in less than a minute without bothering the librarian, who is busy helping some kids with their homework.

Molnar takes the books to his office, where he uses a commercially available reader about the size and heft of a box of Altoids to scan the data from their RFID tags. The reader feeds the data to his computer, which is running software that Molnar ordered from RFID-maker Tagsys. As he waves the reader over a book's spine, ID numbers pop up on his monitor. "I can definitely overwrite these tags," Molnar says. He finds an empty page in the RFID's memory and types "AB." When he scans the book again, we see the barcode with the letters "AB" next to it. (Molnar hastily erases the "AB," saying that he despises library vandalism.) He fumes at the Oakland library's failure to lock the writable area. "I could erase the barcodes and then lock the tags. The library would have to replace them all."

Frank Mussche, Libramation's president, acknowledges that the library's tags were left unlocked. "That's the recommended implementation of our tags," he says. "It makes it easier for libraries to change the data."

For the Oakland Public Library, vulnerability is just one more problem in a buggy system. "This was mostly a pilot program, and it was implemented poorly," says administrative librarian Jerry Garzon. "We've decided to move ahead without Libramation and RFIDs."

But hundreds of libraries have deployed the tags. According to Mussche, Libramation has sold 5 million RFID tags in a "convenient" unlocked state.

[A] stalker could, say, place a cookie on his target's E-ZPass, then return to it a few days later to see which toll plazas the car had crossed (and when).

While it may be hard to imagine why someone other than a determined vandal would take the trouble to change library tags, there are other instances where the small hassle could be worth big bucks. Take the Future Store. Located in Rheinberg, Germany, the Future Store is the world's preeminent test bed of RFID-based retail shopping. All the items in this high tech supermarket have RFID price tags, which allow the store and individual product manufacturers—Gillette, Kraft, Procter & Gamble—to gather instant feedback on what's being bought. Meanwhile, shoppers can check out with a single flash of a reader. In July 2004, *Wired* hailed the store as the "supermarket of the future." A few months later, German security expert Lukas Grunwald hacked the chips.

Grunwald cowrote a program called RFDump, which let him access and alter price chips using a PDA (with an RFID reader) and a PC card antenna. With the store's permission, he and his colleagues strolled the aisles, downloading information from hundreds of sensors. They then showed how easily they could upload one chip's data onto another. "I could download the price of a cheap wine into RFDump," Grunwald says, "then cut and paste it onto the tag of an expensive bottle." The price-switching stunt drew media attention, but the Future Store still didn't lock its price tags. "What we do in the Future Store is purely a test," says the Future Store spokesperson Albrecht von Truchsess. "We don't expect that retailers will use RFID like this at the product level for at least 10 or 15 years." By then, Truchsess thinks, security will be worked out.

Today, Grunwald continues to pull even more elaborate pranks with chips from the Future Store. "I was at a hotel that used smartcards, so I copied one and put the data into my computer," Grunwald says. "Then I used RFDump to upload the room key card data to the price chip on a box of cream cheese from the Future Store. And I opened my hotel room with the cream cheese!"

Aside from pranks, vandalism, and thievery, Grunwald has recently discovered another use for RFID chips: espionage. He programmed RFDump with the ability to place cookies on RFID tags the same way Web sites put cookies on browsers to track returning customers. With this, a stalker could, say, place a cookie on his target's E-ZPass, then return to it a few days later to see which toll plazas the car had crossed (and when). Private citizens and the government could likewise place cookies on library books to monitor who's checking them out.

Brute-Force Attack

In 1997, ExxonMobil equipped thousands of service stations with SpeedPass, which lets customers wave a small RFID device attached to a key chain in front of a pump to pay for gas. Seven years later, three graduate students—Steve Bono, Matthew Green, and Adam Stubblefield—ripped off a station in Baltimore. Using a laptop and a simple RFID broadcasting device, they tricked the system into letting them fill up for free.

The theft was concocted by Avi Rubin's computer science lab at Johns Hopkins University. Rubin's lab is best known for having found massive, hackable flaws in the code running on Diebold's widely adopted electronic voting machines in 2004. Working with RSA Labs manager Juels, the group figured out how to crack the RFID chip in ExxonMobil's SpeedPass. Hacking the tag, which is made by Texas Instruments, is not as simple as breaking into Van Bokkelen's Sandstorm offices with a cloner. The radio signals in these chips, dubbed DST tags, are protected by an encryption cipher that only the chip and the reader can decode. Unfortunately, says Juels, "Texas Instruments used an untested cipher." The Johns Hopkins lab found that the code could be broken with what security geeks call a "brute-force attack," in which a special computer known as a cracker is used to try thousands of password combinations per second until it hits on the right one. Using a home-brewed cracker that cost a few hundred dollars, Juels and the Johns Hopkins team successfully performed a brute-force attack on TI's cipher in only 30 minutes. Compare that to the hundreds of years experts estimate it would take for today's computers to break the publicly available encryption tool SHA-1, which is used to secure credit card transactions on the Internet.

ExxonMobil isn't the only company that uses the Texas Instruments tags. The chips are also commonly used in vehicle security systems. If the reader in the car doesn't detect the chip embedded in the rubbery end of the key handle, the engine won't turn over. But disable the chip and the car can be hotwired like any other.

Bill Allen, director of strategic alliances at Texas Instruments RFID Systems, says he met with the Johns Hopkins team and he isn't worried. "This research was purely academic," Allen says. Nevertheless, he adds, the chips the Johns Hopkins lab tested have already been phased out and replaced with ones that use 128-bit keys, along with stronger public encryption tools, such as SHA-1 and Triple DES.

We believe the new U.S. passport is probably vulnerable to a brute-force attack.

Juels is now looking into the security of the new U.S. passports, the first of which were issued to diplomats this March [2006]. Frank Moss, deputy assistant secretary of state for passport services, claims they are virtually hack-proof. "We've added to the cover an anti-skimming device that prevents anyone from reading the chip unless the passport is open," he says. Data on the chip is encrypted and can't be unlocked without a key printed in machine-readable text on the passport itself.

But Juels still sees problems. While he hasn't been able to work with an actual passport yet, he has studied the government's proposals carefully. "We believe the new U.S. passport is probably vulnerable to a brute-force attack," he says. "The encryption keys in them will depend on passport numbers and birth dates. Because these have a certain degree of structure and guessability, we estimate that the effective key length is at most 52 bits. A special key-cracking machine could probably break a passport key of this length in 10 minutes."

Digital-Age Pickpocket

I'm lying face down on an examination table at UCLA Medical Center, my right arm extended at 90 degrees. Allan Pantuck, a young surgeon wearing running shoes with his lab coat, is inspecting an anesthetized area on the back of my upper arm. He holds up something that looks like a toy gun with a fat silver needle instead of a barrel.

I've decided to personally test-drive what is undoubtedly the most controversial use of RFIDs today—an implantable tag. VeriChip, the only company making FDA-approved tags, boasts on its Web site that "this 'always there' identification can't be lost, stolen, or duplicated." It sells the chips to hospitals as implantable medical ID tags and is starting to promote them as secure-access keys.

Pantuck pierces my skin with the gun, delivering a microchip and antenna combo the size of a grain of long rice. For the rest of my life, a small region on my right arm will emit binary signals that can be converted into a 16-digit number. When Pantuck scans my arm with the VeriChip reader—it looks sort of like the wand clerks use to read barcodes in checkout lines—I hear a quiet beep, and its tiny red LED display shows my ID number.

Three weeks later, I meet the smartcard-intercepting Westhues at a greasy spoon a few blocks from the MIT campus. He's sitting in the corner with a half-finished plate of onion rings, his long blond hair hanging in his face as he hunches over the cloner attached to his computer.

Because the VeriChip uses a frequency close to that of many smartcards, Westhues is pretty sure the cloner will work on my tag. Westhues waves his antenna over my arm and gets some weird readings. Then he presses it lightly against my skin, the way a digital-age pickpocket could in an elevator full of people. He stares at the green waveforms that appear on his computer screen. "Yes, that looks like we got a good reading," he says.

After a few seconds of fiddling, Westhues switches the cloner to Emit and aims its antenna at the reader. *Beep!* My ID number pops up on its screen. So much for implantable IDs being immune to theft. The whole process took 10 minutes. "If you extended the range of this cloner by boosting its power, you could strap it to your leg, and somebody passing the VeriChip reader over your arm would pick up the ID," Westhues says. "They'd never know they hadn't read it from your arm." Using a clone of my tag, as it were, Westhues could access anything the chip was linked to, such as my office door or my medical records.

John Proctor, VeriChip's director of communications, dismisses this problem. "VeriChip is an excellent security system, but it shouldn't be used as a stand-alone," he says. His recommendation: Have someone also check paper IDs.

But isn't the point of an implantable chip that authentication is automatic? "People should know what level of security they're gettting when they inject something into their arm," he says with a half smile.

They should—but they don't. A few weeks after Westhues clones my chip, Cincinnati-based surveillance company City-Watcher announces a plan to implant employees with Veri-Chips. Sean Darks, the company's CEO, touts the chips as "just like a key card." Indeed.

3

RFID Technology Does Not Threaten Privacy

Jay Cline

Jay Cline is a data-privacy specialist at Carlson Companies, which has businesses in travel, hospitality, and marketing and is based in Minneapolis, Minnesota.

The negative hype that surrounds radio-frequency identification (RFID) overshadows reality, and privacy advocates distort the vulnerabilities of RFID technology and its worst-case scenarios. Instead of inviting governments or corporations to spy on unwitting citizens or steal their identities, RFID has the potential to revolutionize commerce and industry. For example, RFID tags can prevent medical mistakes in hospitals, markedly improve automotive maintenance, and streamline postal services. The federal government also stands to save billions of dollars by using RFID inventory-management systems. Regardless of these exceptional benefits, RFID makers must address the public's overblown fears, before the most valuable RFID applications are banned.

The privacy scare surrounding radio frequency identification (RFID) tags is greatly overblown. No company or government agency will be secretly scanning your house, as is feared, to find out what products you've purchased. There is no feasible way to do so. But if RFID chip makers don't soon allay these fears, the escalating public emotion around this issue may effectively ban the most valuable implementations of this remarkable technology.

Jay Cline, "RFID Privacy Scare Is Overblown," *Computerworld*, November 23, 2003. http://computerworld.com. Reproduced by permission.

A Revolution in the Making

What are these mysterious devices? An RFID tag is a microchip the size of a grain of sand that transmits information to a nearby scanner. Typical chips store 96 bits of data and transmit a 125-KHz RF signal. Experts say that capacity is enough to send a product serial number to a scanner a few feet away. Although this capacity is limited, many companies see a revolution in the making.

Hospitals imagine a day when RFID tags will prevent medical errors by transmitting the correct medicine dosages to nurses. Automakers hope similar tags will be able to transmit wear-and-tear information on vehicles before serious problems occur. Postal services see speedier parcel scanning and tracking. Appliance makers and food producers envision faster and more targeted recalls of defective products. Clothing and shoe stores expect faster customer service as RFID tags help identify items of the right size. Clothes manufacturers hope the tags will be able to tell washing machines how to best wash items. The music industry sees the technology reducing piracy, and the federal government hopes RFID tags will help combat counterfeiting and speed bag-checking at airports.

Sound too good to be true? Wal-Mart Stores Inc. and the Pentagon don't think so. They're counting on savings of several billion dollars that RFID tagging will bring them in the form of lower inventory-management costs. Items will no longer need to be individually hand-scanned, expediting product loading, invoicing and customer checkout. Scanners might be placed on shelves to speed restocking and at building exits to prevent theft. These lucrative benefits prompted both organizations to announce . . . that their suppliers must tag their cases and pallets with RFID chips by January 2005 in order to continue doing business with them.

What's the Problem?

The story gets better. Analysts see these dual mandates causing a domino effect throughout the world economy. Procter & Gamble Co.—which sells 17% of its goods through Wal-Mart—expects pallet-level tagging to improve the speed by which it replaces out-of-stock products. P&G sees the technology boosting total revenue by $1.2 billion per year, nearly a 3% increase. Accenture Ltd. estimates that RFID adoption will cause retailers to enjoy an average 3% climb in revenue. Japanese analysts project a worldwide benefit of $276 billion by 2010.

So what's the problem?

Privacy advocates are concerned about tags on products continuing to emit signals in the parking lot, on the road and at home. They're worried that by using charge cards or loyalty cards during checkout, customer identifies could be written to the tags. In the worst scenario, they imagine stalkers and thieves scanning cars and homes for expensive goods and personal information.

It's completely infeasible today for a vehicle to pass down your street and intercept signals from RFID-tagged goods inside your home.

Some companies are already experiencing a customer backlash with their product-level tagging trials. Customers of a New York clothing store recently reacted against the prospect of their clothing sizes being beamed into the air. Wal-Mart reportedly had to cancel a pilot where it tagged packages of high-end razor blades because of strongly negative consumer feedback.

Stories of person-level tagging have only heightened fears of a Big Brother world coming to fruition. In Mexico, some children have reportedly been implanted with RFID chips under the skin so they can be tracked if they're kidnapped. A company in Brazil has supposedly implanted chips into the skin of its employees as their means to gain building access. Closer to home, a school in Buffalo is requiring students to wear RFID-tagged badges around their necks to track arrival times, and a prison is using RFID wristbands to monitor inmates. Some have speculated on the benefit of implanting in people RFID chips containing their medical and criminal histories. With friends like these, does Wal-Mart need any enemies?

The Hype Has Outpaced Reality

The hype around RFID systems has certainly outpaced reality. Manufacturers and retailers have yet to agree on a universal electronic product code, the RFID equivalent of the Universal Product Code used in bar codes. RFID scanning is also far from error-free. But more importantly, RFID signals are so weak that they're easily blocked by metals and dense liquids. It's completely infeasible today for a vehicle to pass down your street and intercept signals from RFID-tagged goods inside your home.

The economics of RFID chips are also limiting how they're used. The most basic read-only chips cost 5 to 50 cents apiece. More complex chips that are read-write and have a wider broadcast range can cost several dollars each. Until these prices approach a penny, RFID chips will be mostly used at the case and pallet level, clear of any personally identifiable activity. Because of these technology and cost limitations, the world will have several years to identify the privacy controls we want to see in RFID systems.

Several companies are already creating these privacy controls. In recent meetings, chip makers and users discussed how the universally accepted principles of data privacy could be built into the RFID process. A top priority was notifying customers that certain items were tagged with these transmitters.

The companies discussed accomplishing this by adopting a common RFID logo to place on product packages. To give customers the ability to turn off the transmitters, the firms plan to make them peel-offs. RSA Security Inc. is also developing a chip that could be worn on watches or bags that would block nearby RFIDs from transmitting certain information. All in all, the RFID privacy ball is rolling.

The gathering storm against RFID tags may soon outpace these positive efforts and make product-level RFID tagging taboo. RFID makers and users should take a time-out from their technical discussions and start talking more with the public about what's going on. Their dreams of big economic returns may well depend on it.

4

RFID Technology May Threaten Privacy and Civil Liberties

American Civil Liberties Union, Consumers Against Supermarket Privacy Invasion and Numbering, Electronic Frontier Foundation, Electronic Privacy Information Center, Junkbusters, Meyda Online, Privacy Activism, Privacy Rights Clearinghouse

The authors of this viewpoint are organizations that aim to defend privacy rights and civil liberties in an era of advancing technologies.

The widespread deployment of radio-frequency identification (RFID), an item-tagging technology that emits radio waves, poses numerous threats to privacy and civil liberties. Because of their minute size, RFID tags can be placed on merchandise, documents, and other objects without a person's knowledge and transmit frequencies that can be picked up by RFID readers up to thirty feet away, which could enable secret human tracking and profiling. RFID proponents contend that these tags can be "killed" or "blocked" to protect privacy, but these measures have neither been proven nor are foolproof; killed tags, for instance, may actually be "asleep" and be reactivated in the future. Ultimately, RFID technology can lead to a climate of ubiquitous surveillance. To prevent this, its usage must be regulated and operated with transparency to all parties, and some RFID practices must be banned outright.

American Civil Liberties Union (ACLU), Consumers Against Supermarket Privacy Invasion and Numbering (CASPIAN), Electronic Frontier Foundation (EFF), Electronic Privacy Information Center (EPIC), Junkbusters, Meyda Online, Privacy Activism, Privacy Rights Clearinghouse, "RFID Position Statement of Consumer Privacy and Civil Liberties Organizations," PrivacyRights.org, November 11, 2003. Reproduced by permission.

Radio Frequency Identification (RFID) is an item-tagging technology with profound societal implications. Used improperly, RFID has the potential to jeopardize consumer privacy, reduce or eliminate purchasing anonymity, and threaten civil liberties.

As organizations and individuals committed to the protection of privacy and civil liberties, we have come together to issue this statement on the deployment of RFID in the consumer environment. In the [following viewpoint], we describe the technology and its uses, define the risks, and discuss potential public policy approaches to mitigate the problems we raise.

RFID tags are tiny computer chips connected to miniature antennae that can be affixed to physical objects. In the most commonly touted applications of RFID, the microchip contains an Electronic Product Code (EPC) with sufficient capacity to provide unique identifiers for all items produced worldwide. When an RFID reader emits a radio signal, tags in the vicinity respond by transmitting their stored data to the reader. With passive (battery-less) RFID tags, read-range can vary from less than an inch to 20–30 feet, while active (self-powered) tags can have a much longer read range. Typically, the data is sent to a distributed computing system involved in, perhaps, supply chain management or inventory control.

Threats to Privacy and Civil Liberties

While there are beneficial uses of RFID, some attributes of the technology could be deployed in ways that threaten privacy and civil liberties:

Hidden placement of tags. RFID tags can be embedded into/onto objects and documents without the knowledge of the individual who obtains those items. As radio waves travel easily and silently through fabric, plastic, and other materials, it is possible to read RFID tags sewn into clothing or affixed to objects contained in purses, shopping bags, suitcases, and more.

If personal identity were linked with unique RFID tag numbers, individuals could be profiled and tracked without their knowledge or consent.

Unique identifiers for all objects worldwide. The Electronic Product Code potentially enables every object on earth to have its own unique ID. The use of unique ID numbers could lead to the creation of a global item registration system in which every physical object is identified and linked to its purchaser or owner at the point of sale or transfer.

Massive data aggregation. RFID deployment requires the creation of massive databases containing unique tag data. These records could be linked with personal identifying data, especially as computer memory and processing capacities expand.

Hidden readers. Tags can be read from a distance, not restricted to line of sight, by readers that can be incorporated invisibly into nearly any environment where human beings or items congregate. RFID readers have already been experimentally embedded into floor tiles, woven into carpeting and floor mats, hidden in doorways, and seamlessly incorporated into retail shelving and counters, making it virtually impossible for a consumer to know when or if he or she was being "scanned."

Individual tracking and profiling. If personal identity were linked with unique RFID tag numbers, individuals could be profiled and tracked without their knowledge or consent. For example, a tag embedded in a shoe could serve as a de facto identifier for the person wearing it. Even if item-level information remains generic, identifying items people wear or carry could associate them with, for example, particular events like political rallies.

Framework of RFID Rights and Responsibilities

This framework respects businesses' interest in tracking products in the supply chain, but emphasizes individuals' rights to not be tracked within stores and after products are purchased. To mitigate the potential harmful consequences of RFID to individuals and to society, we recommend a three-part framework. First, RFID must undergo a formal technology assessment, and RFID tags should not be affixed to individual consumer products until such assessment takes place. Second, RFID implementation must be guided by Principles of Fair Information Practice. Third, certain uses of RFID should be flatly prohibited.

Technology assessment. RFID must be subject to a formal technology assessment process, sponsored by a neutral entity, perhaps similar to the model established by the now defunct Congressional Office of Technology Assessment. The process must be multi-disciplinary, involving all stakeholders, including consumers.

Principles of Fair Information Practice. RFID technology and its implementation must be guided by strong principles of fair information practices (FIPs). The eight-part Privacy Guidelines of the Organisation for Economic Cooperation and Development (OECD) provides a useful model. We agree that the following minimum guidelines, based in part on these principles, must be adhered to while the larger assessment of RFID's societal implications takes place:

Openness, or transparency. RFID users must make public their policies and practices involving the use and maintenance of RFID systems, and there should be no secret databases. Individuals have a right to know when products or items in the retail environment contain RFID tags or readers. They also have the right to know the technical specifications of those devices. Labeling must be clearly displayed and easily understood. Any tag reading that occurs in the retail environment must be transparent to all parties. There should be no tag-reading in secret.

Purpose specification. RFID users must give notice of the purposes for which tags and readers are used.

Collection limitation. The collection of information should be limited to that which is necessary for the purpose at hand.

Accountability. RFID users are responsible for implementation of this technology and the associated data. RFID users should be legally responsible for complying with the principles. An accountability mechanism must be established. There must be entities in both industry and government to whom individuals can complain when these provisions have been violated.

Security safeguards. There must be security and integrity in transmission, databases, and system access. These should be verified by outside, third-party, publicly disclosed assessment.

RFID should never be employed in a fashion to eliminate or reduce anonymity. For instance, RFID should not be incorporated into currency.

RFID Practices that Should Be Flatly Prohibited

Merchants must be prohibited from forcing or coercing customers into accepting live or dormant RFID tags in the products they buy.

There should be no prohibition on individuals to detect RFID tags and readers and disable tags on items in their possession.

RFID must not be used to track individuals absent informed and written consent of the data subject. Human tracking is inappropriate, either directly or indirectly, through clothing, consumer goods, or other items.

RFID should never be employed in a fashion to eliminate or reduce anonymity. For instance, RFID should not be incorporated into currency.

Acceptable Uses of RFID

We have identified several examples of "acceptable" uses of RFID in which consumer-citizens are not subjected to "live" RFID tags and their attendant risks.

Tracking of pharmaceuticals from the point of manufacture to the point of dispensing. RFID tags could help ensure that these critical goods are not counterfeit, that they are handled properly, and that they are dispensed appropriately. RFID tags contained on or in the pharmaceutical containers should be physically removed or permanently disabled before being sold to consumers.

Tracking of manufactured goods from the point of manufacture to the location where they will be shelved for sale. RFID tags could help ensure that products are not lost or stolen as they move through the supply chain. The tags could also assure the goods are handled appropriately. Tags should be confined to the outside of product packaging (not embedded in the packaging) and be permanently destroyed before consumers interact with them in the store.

Detection of items containing toxic substances when they are delivered to the landfill. For example, when a personal computer is brought to the landfill, a short-range RFID tag could communicate toxic content to a reader at the landfill. It is important to underscore that uses such as the landfill example do not require—and should not entail—item-level unique identifiers. The RFID tag would, rather, emit a generic recycling or waste disposal message.

We are requesting manufacturers and retailers to agree to a voluntary moratorium on the item-level RFID tagging of consumer items until a formal technology assessment process involving all stakeholders, including consumers, can take place.

Further, the development of this technology must be guided by a strong set of Principles of Fair Information Practice, ensuring that meaningful consumer control is built into the implementation of RFID. Finally, some uses of RFID technology are inappropriate in a free society, and should be flatly prohibited. Society should not wait for a crisis involving RFID before exerting oversight.

Although not examined in this [viewpoint], we must also grapple with the civil liberties implications of governmental adoption of RFID. The Department of Defense has issued an RFID mandate to its suppliers, schools and libraries . . . have begun implementing RFID, the EU and the Japanese government have considered the use of RFID in currency, and British law enforcement has expressed an interest in using RFID as an investigative tool. As an open democratic society, we must adopt a strong policy framework based on Principles of Fair Information Practice to guide governmental implementation of RFID.

Limitations of RFID Technology: Myths Debunked

The following technological limitations have been proposed as reasons why consumers should not be concerned about RFID deployment at this time. We address each perceived limitation in turn, and explain why in themselves, these limitations cannot be relied upon as adequate consumer protection from the risks outlined above.

1. Read-range distances are not sufficient to allow for consumer surveillance.

RFID tags have varying read ranges depending on their antenna size, transmission frequency, and whether they are passive or active. Some passive RFID tags have read ranges of less than one inch. Other RFID tags can be read at distances of 20 feet or more. Active RFID tags theoretically have very long ranges. Currently, most RFID tags envisioned for consumer products are passive with read ranges of under 5 feet.

Contrary to some assertions, tags with shorter read ranges are not necessarily less effective for tracking human beings or items associated with them. In fact, in some cases a shorter read range can be more powerful. For example, if there were an interest in tracking individuals through their shoes as they come within range of a floor reader, a two-inch read range would be preferable to a two-foot read range. Such a short range would help minimize interference with other tags in the vicinity, and help assure the capture of only the pertinent tag positioned directly on the reader.

2. Reader devices not prevalent enough to enable seamless human tracking.

The developers of RFID technology envision a world where RFID readers form a "pervasive global network." It does not take a ubiquitous reader network to track objects or the people associated with them. For example, automobiles traveling up and down Interstate 95 can be tracked without placing RFID readers every few feet. They need only be positioned at the entrance and exit ramps. Similarly, to track an individual's whereabouts in a given town, it is not necessary to position a reader device every ten feet in that town, as long as readers are present at strategic locations such as building entrances.

3. Limited information contained on tags.

Some RFID proponents defend the technology by pointing out that the tags associated with most consumer products will contain only a serial number. However, the number can actually be used as a reference number that corresponds to information contained on one or more Internet-connected databases. This means that the data associated with that number is theoretically unlimited, and can be augmented as new information is collected.

For example, when a consumer purchases a product with an EPC-compliant RFID tag, information about the consumer who purchased it could be added to the database automatically. Additional information could be logged in the file as the consumer goes about her business: "Entered the Atlanta courthouse at 12:32 PM," "At Mobil gas station at 2:14 PM," etc. Such data could be accessed by anyone with access to such a database, whether authorized or not.

4. Passive tags cannot be tracked by satellite.

The passive RFID tags envisioned for most consumer products do not have their own power, meaning they must be activated and queried by nearby reader devices. Thus, by themselves, passive tags do not have the ability to communicate via satellites.

However, the information contained on passive RFID tags could be picked up by ambient reader devices which in turn transmit their presence and location to satellites. Such technology has already been used to track the real-time location of products being shipped on moving vehicles through the North American supply chain.

In addition, active RFID tags with their own power source can be enabled with direct satellite transmitting capability. At the present time such tags are far too expensive to be used on most consumer products, but this use is not inconceivable as technology advances and prices fall.

5. High cost of tags make them prohibitive for wide-scale deployment.

RFID developers point to the "high cost" of RFID tags as a way to assuage consumer fears about the power of such tags. However, as technology improves and prices fall, we predict that more and more consumer products will carry tags and that those tags will become smaller and more sophisticated. We predict that the trend will follow the trends of other technical products like computers and calculators.

A Critique of Proposed Industry Solutions

The RFID industry has suggested a variety of solutions to address the dangers posed by RFID tagging of consumer products. Among them are killing the tags at point of sale, the use of "blocker tags," and the "closed system." We examine each strategy in turn.

Killing Tags at Point of Sale

Some have proposed that the RFID tag problem could be solved by killing the tags at the point of sale, rendering them inoperable. There are several reasons why we do not believe this approach alone and without other protections will adequately protect consumer privacy:

Killing tags after purchase does not address in-store tracking of consumers.

To date, nearly all consumer privacy invasion associated with RFID tagging of consumer products has occurred within the retail environment, long before consumers reached the checkout counter where chips could be killed. Examples include:

Close-up photographs were taken of consumers as they picked up RFID-tagged packages of Gillette razor products from store shelves equipped with Auto-ID Center "smart shelf" technology.

A video camera trained on a Wal-Mart cosmetics shelf in Oklahoma enabled distant Procter and Gamble executives to observe unknowing customers as they interacted with RFID-tagged lipsticks.

Plans are underway to tag books and magazines with RFID devices to allow detailed in-store observation of people browsing reading materials. This potential was demonstrated recently at the Tokyo International Book Fair 2003. According to Japan's *Nikkei Electronic News*, "By placing tag readers on the shelves of bookstores, the new system allows booksellers to gain information such as the range of books a shopper has browsed, how many times a particular title was picked up and even the length of time spent flipping through each book."

If RFID tags are allowed to become ubiquitous in consumer products, removing the kill option could enable the instant creation of a surveillance society.

We recognize the need for stores to control shoplifting and make general assessments to enhance operations. However, monitoring and recording the detailed behaviors of consumers without their consent, even if only within the store, violates Principles of Fair Information Practice.

Tags can appear to be "killed" when they are really "asleep" and can be reactivated.

Some RFID tags have a "dormant" or "sleep" state that could be set, making it appear to the average consumer that the tag had been killed. It would be possible for retailers and others to claim to have killed a tag when in reality they had simply rendered it dormant. It would be possible to later reactivate and read such a "dormant" tag.

The tag-killing option could be easily halted by government directive.

It would take very little for a security threat or a change in governmental policies to remove the kill-tag option. If RFID tags are allowed to become ubiquitous in consumer products, removing the kill option could enable the instant creation of a surveillance society.

Retailers might offer incentives or disincentives to consumers to encourage them to leave tags active.

Consumers wishing to kill tags could be required to perform additional steps or undergo burdensome procedures, such as waiting in line for a "killer kiosk" and then being required to kill the tags themselves. Consumers who choose to kill the tags might not enjoy the same discounts or benefits as other consumers, or might not be allowed the same return policies. In many areas of privacy law, this retailer incentive is recognized, and there are legislative prohibitions against inducing the consumer to waive their privacy rights.

The creation of two classes of consumers.

If killing tags requires conscious effort on the part of consumers, many will fail to do so out of fear, ignorance, or lack of time. Many will choose *not* to kill the tags if doing so is inconvenient. (The current "killer kiosk" requires loading one item at a time, a lengthy and time-consuming process.) This would create two classes of consumers: those who "care enough" to kill the RFID tags in their products and those who don't. Being a member of either class could have negative ramifications.

The blocker tag might encourage the proliferation of RFID devices by giving consumers a false sense of security.

Blocker Tags

RFID blocker tags are electronic devices that should theoretically disrupt the transmission of all or select information contained on RFID tags. The proposed blocker tag might be embedded in a shopping bag, purse, or watch that is carried or worn near tags with information consumers want blocked.

Blocker tags are still theoretical.

According to our understanding, the blocker tag does not yet exist. Until a blocker tag is built and tested, there is no way to know how effective it will be and whether it can be technically defeated.

Encourages the widespread deployment of RFID tags.

The blocker tag might encourage the proliferation of RFID devices by giving consumers a false sense of security. While the proposed invention is an ingenious idea, it's one that could be banned or be underutilized if consumers become complacent. It's also possible that such an electronic device could be technically defeated either purposefully or because it stops functioning naturally.

The blocker tag could be banned by government directive or store policy.

Consumers could lose the right to use blocker tag devices if the government deems that knowing what people are wearing or carrying is necessary for national security. They might disallow the devices altogether or name selective spaces in which blocker tags would be disallowed. It is not inconceivable to imagine a ban on such devices in airports or public buildings, for example.

Retail stores might ban blocker tags if they believe the tags might be used to circumvent security measures or if they believe knowing details about consumers is valuable in their marketing efforts.

Once RFID tags and readers are ubiquitous in the environment, a full or partial ban on a privacy device like the blocker tag would leave consumers exposed and vulnerable to privacy invasion.

Adds a burden to consumers.

A blocker tag shifts the burden of protecting privacy away from the manufacturers and retailers and places it on the shoulders of consumers. In addition, busy consumers might forget to carry blocker devices or forget to implement them, especially if additional steps are required to make them effective.

Fails to protect consumers once products are separated from the blocker tag.

Blocker tags theoretically work only when they are close to the items they are designed to "conceal" from RFID reader devices. Once items are out of the range of the blocking device, consumers would be exposed and vulnerable to privacy invasion. For example, a consumer might buy a sweater and feel that the information on the embedded RFID tag is unexposed because she is carrying it home in a bag impregnated with a blocker device. However, once she removes that sweater from the bag and wears it in range of a reader device, information from that tag could be gleaned.

The creation of two classes of consumers.

Like the kill-tag feature, blocker tags will also likely create two classes of consumers, those who block tags and those who do not.

Closed System

Industry proponents argue that when RFID applications are confined to closed systems, the data is only accessible to those within the system and those with a government mandate (perhaps via legislation such as the Communications Access to Law Enforcement Act [CALEA]). Therefore they argue, society-wide profiling and tracking are not likely.

An example of a current closed application is RFID in libraries. *The Grapes of Wrath* in Library X has a different code than the same book in Library Y.

Whereas today RFID applications are confined to closed systems, there will be great incentives to standardize product level tagging. Publishers, for example, may someday ship books to libraries and bookstores with writable tags. Each copy of *The Grapes of Wrath* will contain a portion of its EPC code that is the same as every other copy. The library will be able to customize the remainder of the code to suit its own inventory control purposes.

Even if closed systems remain closed, their lack of transparency makes them troubling from a privacy perspective. Because details about closed systems might not be readily available, consumers could have difficulty obtaining the information necessary to assess privacy risks and protect themselves.

We appreciate that industry proponents are making an effort to address consumer privacy and civil liberties concerns associated with RFID technology. However, while we believe the proposed solutions are offered in the proper spirit, they provide inadequate protection. Until appropriate solutions are developed and agreed upon, we believe it is improper to subject consumers to the dangers of RFID technology through item-level consumer product tagging.

5

RFID Technology Can Be Beneficial While Protecting Consumer Privacy

Ari Juels

Ari Juels is director and chief scientist of RSA Laboratories, which is based in Bedford, Massachusetts. Juels is also coinventor of two RFID privacy technologies, the privacy bit and blocker tag.

The terms radio-frequency identification (RFID) and consumer privacy go hand in hand. Although there are legitimate privacy concerns regarding the tiny radio-wave-emitting tags, RFID's main opponents paint the privacy issue in black-and-white while slighting the technology's innovations. Therefore, "killing" RFID tags is upheld as a solution, but it also undermines their consumer benefits, such as RFID-enhanced home appliances and merchandise returns without receipts. In fact, killing tags will kill their unrealized potential—including RFID's integration with the Internet. Moreover, there are viable alternatives that can balance privacy with utility: an RFID tag "privacy" bit can be turned on and off and "blocker tags" can confer protection to consumers from RFID readers. The lessons learned from the Internet will also help pave the way to RFID security.

RFID privacy inflames passions as few other technological issues can. Readers . . . are familiar with the enormous swirl of media attention around the topic. A statistic compiled

Ari Juels, "A Bit of Privacy," *RFID Journal*, May 2, 2005. http://rfidjournal.com. Copyright © 2005 RFID Journal LLC. Reproduced by permission.

by Ravi Pappu of ThingMagic summarizes the situation nicely: Of the Web pages returned by a Google search on the term "RFID" in late 2003, some 42 percent also contained the word "privacy." If item-level RFID tagging comes to pass, there is no gainsaying the privacy concerns it will bring. There is a real possibility of constellations of small wireless devices promiscuously emitting personal information. Some of the backlash against RFID, however, has assumed a form that is purely dramatic. Terms like "spy-chips," for example, neatly encapsulate the anxieties of a certain class of RFID opponent. But they distort any meaningful discussion of the uses of RFID, deny its benefits and cast privacy as a black-and-white issue.

The RFID community largely sees through extreme claims about privacy. What it overlooks is the dramatic nature of its own response. To address the problem of consumer privacy, RFID vendors and users have designed EPC tags of the Generation 2 variety so that they can be "killed." Killing means rendering tags permanently inoperative at the point of sale. This solution to the privacy problem—preemptive capital punishment for RFID tags, as it were—is psychologically gratifying; it is simple and direct. But it too casts the question of consumer privacy in black-and-white terms. The practice of killing RFID tags presupposes that their dangers to consumers are otherwise uncontrollable. The collateral damage would be extensive.

Killing Tags, Killing Visions

Killing tags would kill many visions of RFID benefit for consumers. If consumers possess only dead RFID tags, then smart appliances such as RFID-enhanced refrigerators, ovens and washing machines will be unrealizable. Likewise, RFID systems to aid the elderly with medication compliance and navigation of their environments will be more difficult to deploy. The killing of tags would preclude many other possibilities for consumers, like item returns in retail shops without receipts (not to mention the concomitant benefits to industry, like refined quality-control information), retrieval of lost items, automated product-part searches and so forth.

If RFID tags are killed, perhaps the greatest loss will be the innovations that have yet to be dreamed of. The Internet extended the reach of computing systems in ways that were unimaginable a decade or two ago. RFID will extend the Internet, and give rise to an infrastructure in which computing systems possess a new awareness of the world around them. Live RFID tags in the hands of consumers could open the sluices for another torrent of invention.

To construct a broad RFID infrastructure safely, a balance needs to be struck between privacy and utility. The benefits of tags must be readily available, but so too should the means for restricting their emission of information. The aim of this article is to describe the privacy bit, a simple technological tool that helps achieve such a balance. The privacy bit may be viewed as a natural extension of an existing technology known as electronic article surveillance, or EAS. EAS can serve as a conceptual and technical bridge for the privacy bit.

Electronic Article Surveillance

EAS is commonplace and familiar to most consumers. Many articles in shops—from books to hair driers—bear small tags for theft prevention. At the point of sale, sales clerks deactivate these tags, generally by passing them over demagnetizing blocks. When a patron removes a tagged article without payment—or a sales clerk neglects to deactivate a tag properly—an alarm sounds at the shop exit.

EAS tags and RFID tags are similar in form. Inasmuch as they both track the whereabouts of objects, they are similar in function as well. The marriage of the two technologies is therefore natural, and some vendors are already integrating

EAS functionality into their RFID tags. . . . One way to implement EAS in an RFID system is to deactivate tags at the point of sale, as is done today.

An alternative is to set aside a logical bit on the RFID tag. This bit is initially off when items are in the shop. The bit is flipped to the on position to deactivate a tag at the point of sale. To allow purchased articles to pass without activating an alarm, the antitheft gates at shop exits disregard tags whose bit is on. If live RFID tags and EAS systems are to coexist, bit flipping is the only viable approach.

Like an EAS tag, an on/off bit in an RFID tag can be informative: It indicates whether an item belongs to the shop or to a consumer. Theft prevention is therefore only one possible use for this bit. As we shall explain, this bit can also serve to protect consumers against unwanted RFID scanning. Indeed, this bit is what we shall refer to as the privacy bit.

With proper RFID reader configuration, the privacy bit strikes an attractive balance between privacy and utility.

The Privacy Bit

If RFID readers in shops refrain from scanning private tags, i.e., those tags whose privacy bit is turned on, then a good measure of consumer privacy will already be in place. Tags belonging to consumers in this case will be invisible to shops. At the same time, tags on items on shelves and storage rooms, i.e., those that have not yet been purchased, will be perfectly visible. The privacy bit will not impact normal industrial use of RFID.

In some locations, of course, it will be desirable and appropriate for RFID readers to scan private tags. Home appliances should contain RFID readers capable of scanning private tags. RFID readers that scan tags for item returns in shops might likewise have this capability, if consumers want it. (These readers, however, would need special restrictions on their use and, ideally, physical protections like metallic shielding and visible identifiers.)

With proper RFID reader configuration, the privacy bit strikes an attractive balance between privacy and utility. To ensure this balance, there is a need to enforce proper reader configuration and to defend against rogue readers used intentionally to infringe privacy.

A palette of technological tools can help. To support these tools, there needs to be a supplementary (and optional-to-deploy) RFID read command, which we might call private-read. A tag with its privacy bit turned off will respond to an ordinary read command; a tag with its privacy bit turned on will respond only to a private-read command.

The private-read command enables a few different approaches to privacy enforcement:

Audit. The simplest way to ensure the correct configuration of RFID readers is to check up on them. Thanks to the private-read command, this is a simple matter. In order to scan private tags, a reader must transmit a private-read command; it thereby publicly broadcasts its behavior. Special-purpose audit devices can detect the emission of a private-read command and identify readers that scan private tags. In fact, a properly configured RFID reading device can itself audit other readers; RFID readers might check up on one another. Once mobile phones come equipped with the right RFID functionality—a seemingly inevitable trend—they might alert their owners to the fact of private scanning taking place, facilitating a kind of citizens' watch network for RFID privacy.

Blocking. Reader auditing detects violations as they occur, or after the fact. A technological tool known as a blocker tag or blocker, on the other hand, can prevent privacy violations before they occur. A blocker effectively jams readers that emit private-read commands. In a nutshell, when it detects a private-read command, it simulates all possible RFID tags in the world, rendering the reader incapable of communicating with other tags. . . .

By carrying a blocker, a consumer can ensure against scanning of her personal possessions. When she wants private items to be scanned—in the home for example—she need merely remove her blocker tag from their vicinity. For example, if the consumer has a blocker tag mounted on the outside of her pocketbook, it will confer privacy protection while she is walking in the street. When she puts her RFID-tagged garments in a smart, RFID-enabled washing machine, though, the blocker will have no effect.

Blocker tags are just a research concept at present. They could, however, assume a form similar in size and cost to ordinary tags, and might even be embedded in shopping bags. Alternatively, to ensure easier management and more consistent signal strength, a blocker might be realized in a powered device like a mobile phone.

Blockers, of course, are selective in the sense that they have no impact on the scanning of tags whose privacy bit is off. This special, critical feature means that blockers would have no effect on ordinary industrial RFID readers.

Policy. Technology works most effectively in concert with well-crafted policy. Laws or guidelines around the appropriate use of private RFID scanning would benefit technological aids like the privacy bit. Researchers with the Auto-ID Lab at the University of St. Gallen and ETH Zurich have enunciated ideas similar in spirit to the privacy bit, and have investigated both enforcement via audit devices and the relationship of their ideas to the Organization for Economic Cooperation and Development's guidelines for protecting personal information. . . .

The privacy bit is a technical springboard for privacy enhancement. No doubt technologists and policy makers will be able to develop many other ways to exploit and build upon it.

Technical Realization of the Privacy Bit

Realization of the privacy bit as a supplement to EPCglobal's Gen 2 standard would be technically straightforward. The privacy bit would of course reside in an EPC tag as an additional logical bit of memory. (As it would serve only to control the response of the tag to the read and private-read commands, the privacy bit would not need to be memory-mapped.)

The kill command in the EPCglobal standard then provides a ready vehicle for secure flipping of the privacy bit. The standard designates three bits within the kill command whose function is as yet unspecified. (They are "reserved for future use.") One of these three might serve as a privacy-control bit. It would function as follows. When a reader issues the kill command with the privacy-control bit off, the result is an ordinary kill operation that permanently disables the tag. When a reader issues the kill command with the privacy-control bit on, however, no killing takes place. Instead, the kill command merely flips the privacy bit. For the easiest and most inexpensive deployment, the privacy bit could be one-time writeable, that is, subject to a single flip from off to on. For situations that require reuse (e.g., for EPC-tagged library books), tags might support multiple changes to the privacy bit.

The EPCglobal standard requires that the kill command be activated by means of numerical code unique to each tag. The operation of flipping the privacy bit would naturally inherit this security feature. Such protection is important, as wanton flipping of privacy bits would be just as bad as wanton killing of tags.

As an option in the EPCglobal standard, the privacy bit would have one very attractive feature: It would impose no cost on tag vendors that choose not to implement it. A vendor could produce tags that do not contain a privacy bit and do not recognize the private-read command (or, alternatively, always recognize it). Such tags would function normally in commercial environments, and might be killed at the point of sale, if desired.

We are now well placed to avoid the mistakes of the wired world as we lay the foundations for a new wireless one.

A Stitch in Time Saves Nine

There is a broad recognition in the RFID industry that tagging of retail articles is some years away. It is tempting to put off contemplation of the privacy bit and kindred ideas for consumer privacy protection in favor of more immediate RFID deployment problems. This would be shortsighted.

While item-level tagging may be a distant prospect, pivotal policy discussions on RFID privacy are afoot. A recent flurry of state-level legislation has focused on RFID; early bills have died, but pending ones may not. Attention within the governments of the United States and the European Union is mounting. The RFID industry must demonstrate forethought if it is to avoid the heavy hand of legislative regulation.

While EPC tags may not percolate into retail settings in the near term, consumers are already carrying RFID tags that pose privacy and security problems. Automobile immobilizers, proximity cards, and Speedpass tokens, all RFID tags in the broad sense of the term, are already commonplace. They render the problems of privacy and security both palpable and immediate to consumers. E-passports and other RFID-enabled identity cards loom on the horizon. Some libraries have already started to tag books with RFID; it is only a matter of time before video stores and other rental operations do so. (Note that for loaned or rented items, tag killing is unworkable, as a tag must last the lifetime of the article it is attached to. The privacy bit or a like solution will be essential.)

Most vital is the problem of legacy infrastructure. The RFID systems that we design today will last for decades; we will have to live with the security choices we make now. The security problems that bedevil the Internet today are instructive. Ten or 20 years ago, viruses, spyware and phishing were concepts of largely academic interest. Security features that might have prevented these problems seemed unjustified in the short term, and the architects of the Internet omitted them. The resulting flaws are today threatening to cripple Internet commerce. (In 2004, phishing in the U.S. alone produced industry losses estimated at $1.2 billion.) These security problems on the Internet are costly, but there is a cause for hope: The software by which users connect to the Internet can be updated or patched. Retooling billions of little wireless hardware devices would be a more strenuous exercise.

Mistakes in Internet security have provided excellent schooling for the RFID community. We are now well placed to avoid the mistakes of the wired world as we lay the foundations for a new wireless one. It is to be hoped that EPCglobal and other industry bodies will rise to the challenge, and that the privacy bit and kindred concepts will smooth the way.

6

RFID Technology Enhances Passport Security

U.S. Department of State

The U.S. Department of State is the agency of foreign affairs of the federal government.

Since August 2007, newly issued U.S. passports are embedded with radio-frequency identification (RFID) tags that electronically store the data provided on its information page. In addition, each tag contains a biometric identifier, in the form of a digital image, for the use of face recognition technology and a digital signature that safeguards the integrity of the data. Electronic passports automate identity verification, speed up immigration inspections, and enhance border protection. With privacy and identity security in mind, effective measures are in place to deter unauthorized viewing, copying, and altering of passport data stored in RFID tags. A built-in feature in these tags also thwarts the potential for human tracking.

An Electronic Passport is the same as a traditional passport with the addition of a small integrated circuit (or "chip") embedded in the back cover. The chip stores:

- The same data visually displayed on the data page of the passport;

U.S. Department of State, "The U.S. Electronic Passport Frequently Asked Questions," 2007. http://travel.state.gov/passport.

- A biometric identifier in the form of a digital image of the passport photograph, which will facilitate the use of face recognition technology at ports-of-entry;

- The unique chip identification number; and

- A digital signature to protect the stored data from alteration.

Special Features

What is a Biometric? Which one does the new Electronic Passport use?

A biometric or biometric identifier is a measurable physical or behavioral characteristic of an individual, which can be used to verify the identity of that individual or to compare against other entries when stored in a database. Biometrics include face recognition, fingerprints, and iris scans. The U.S. Electronic Passport uses the digital image of the passport photograph as the biometric identifier that is used with face recognition technology to verify the identity of the passport bearer. . . .

What are the special features of an Electronic Passport?

The special features of an Electronic Passport are:

- Securely stored biographical information and digital image that are identical to the information that is visually displayed in the passport;

- Contactless chip technology that allows the information stored in an Electronic Passport to be read by special chip readers at a close distance.

- Uses digital signature technology to verify the authenticity of the data stored on the chip. This technology is commonly used in credit cards and other secure documents using integrated circuits or chips.

How does an Electronic Passport facilitate travel?

The Electronic Passport facilitates travel by allowing:

- Automated identity verification;

- Faster immigration inspections; and

- Greater border protection and security.

The Electronic Passport is designed to function for the passport's full validity period under normal use.

As a security measure, Congress has legislated that all countries participating in the Visa Waiver Program with the United States must issue passports with integrated circuits (chips), to permit storage of at least a digital image of the passport photograph for use with face recognition technology. The U.S. is doing so on a reciprocal basis and will comply with the latest international standards established for secure travel documents.

What countries will issue an Electronic Passport?

Several other nations have begun or will begin to issue e-passports. The Visa Waiver Program countries have already done so.

What happens if an Electronic Passport is lost or stolen?

Any passport that is lost or stolen should be reported immediately. U.S. passports reported lost or stolen are invalidated and can no longer be used for travel. . . .

What is the Electronic Passport logo and what does it mean?

The Electronic Passport logo is the international symbol for an electronic passport. It signifies that the passport contains an integrated circuit or chip on which data about the passport and passport bearer is stored. The logo will be displayed at border inspection lanes at all airports and transit parts equipped with special data readers for Electronic Passports.

Can a previously issued passport still be used for travel as long as it is still valid?

Yes. Previously issued passports that are still valid can be used for travel.

Can the new electronic passport be amended, for example, if I change my name?

No. The new electronic passports cannot be amended. If you change your name, need to extend a limited passport, or need a correction in the descriptive information, you will have to get a new passport. Within the first year after issuance, the new passport will be issued without additional payment of the passport fee. After one year, fees will be assessed for the new passport.

Can a request be made for a new passport to be issued without a chip?

No. Since August 2007, all domestic passport agencies and centers issue only e-passports.

One of the simplest measures for preventing unauthorized reading of e-passports is to add RF blocking material to the cover of an e-passport.

Diminishing Nefarious Acts

Will someone be able to read or access the information on the chip without my knowledge (also known as skimming or eavesdropping)?

We feel that it would be good to point out what we have done to diminish the known nefarious acts of "skimming" data from the chip, "eavesdropping" on communications between the chip and reader, "tracking" passport holders, and "cloning" the passport chip in order to facilitate identity theft crimes.

Skimming is the act of obtaining data from an unknowing end user who is not willingly submitting the sample at that time. Eavesdropping is the interception of information as it moves electronically between the chip and the chip reader.

"Skimming." The Department is using an embedded metallic element in our passports. One of the simplest measures for preventing unauthorized reading of e-passports is to add RF blocking material to the cover of an e-passport. Before such a passport can be read, it has to be physically opened. It is a simple and effective method for reducing the opportunity for unauthorized reading of the passport at times when the holder does not expect it.

"Skimming" and "Eavesdropping." We have adopted Basic Access Control (BAC) to minimize the risk of "skimming" and "eavesdropping." Basic Access Control requires that the initial interaction between the embedded microchip in the passport and the border control reader include protocols for setting up the secure communication channel. To ensure that only authorized RFID readers can read data, Basic Access Control stores a pair of secret cryptographic keys in the passport chip. When a reader attempts to scan the passport, it engages in a challenge-response protocol that proves knowledge of the pair of keys and derives a session key. If authentication is successful, the passport releases its data contents; otherwise, the reader is deemed unauthorized and the passport refuses read access. This control would require the receiving state to read the passport machine-readable zone (MRZ) to unlock and read the data on the chip. The MRZ information is used for computing the encryption and message authentication keys used for the "secure" exchange. BAC mollifies the possibility of both "skimming" and "eavesdropping."

"Tracking." A chip that is protected by the BAC mechanism denies access to its contents unless the inspection system can prove that it is authorized to access the chip. However, these chips still allow the Unique Identifier (UID) to be communicated with the reader, which could theoretically allow the document bearer to be "tracked." To prevent the use of the UID for "tracking," the Department is using a Random UID feature. A RUID presents a different UID each time the chip is accessed. In order to be considered random, the e-passport must present an RUID that cannot be associated with UIDs used in sessions that precede or follow the current session. Each chip uses its onboard hardware random number generator (RNG) module, thereby utilizing a true RNG base to derive a RUID.

"Cloning." It is possible to substitute the chip of an e-passport with a fake chip storing the data copied from the chip of another e-passport. However, the simplest way to mitigate this threat is to verify that the chip data belongs to the presented e-passport. This can be done by comparing the data stored on the chip to data on the e-passport's data page. If the photos and biographical date matches and the passport does not appear to have been tampered with (is not counterfeited), then the e-passport and the data stored on the chip can be considered to be belonging together. Additionally, the introduction of Public Key Infrastructure (PKI) into travel documents provides, for the first time, the means of automatically (without human intervention) confirming that the person presenting the travel document, is the same person shown on the data page, and on the chip, with the assurance that the data was put there by the issuing authority and that the data has not been changed.

Can the information on the chip be altered and how is the information protected from being accessed by an unauthorized reader?

The new passports use Public Key Infrastructure (PKI) technology that prevents the information stored on the chip from being altered. The e-passport and the use of the PKI digital signature stands to benefit the legitimate traveler. It provides a more sophisticated means to confirm that the traveler is the rightful holder of the passport and that the passport is authentic, thus deterring would-be passport/identity thieves. Use of the PKI to validate and authenticate the data in the chip supports passport inspection and would strengthen border control systems.

What will happen if my Electronic passport fails at a port-of-entry?

The chip in the passport is just one of the many security features of the new passport. If the chip fails, the passport remains a valid travel document until its expiration date. The bearer will continue to be processed by the port-of-entry officer as if he/she had a passport without a chip.

RFID Technology May Not Protect Passports and Enhance Security

Donald Davis

Donald Davis is editorial director of Chicago-based publishing company Vertical Web Media. He is former editor of Card Technology, *a smart cards and personal identification industry magazine.*

In the next decade, a half a billion passports from some forty or so nations will be embedded with data-transmitting radio-frequency identification (RFID) tags, with the aim to improve personal identification as well as deter passport counterfeiting and terrorism. Despite the new possibilities, much can go awry with these electronic passports. RFID tags and readers manufactured by different vendors may not be compatible and cause travel delays and tie up border crossings. The security of sensitive data in electronic passports is also uncertain. Furthermore, in a worst-case scenario, terrorists equipped with sensors may be able read RFID-tagged passports and target specific nationals for attack. Even though improvements are being made, electronic passports may fall short of expectations.

Some 40 countries are preparing to introduce in [2006] new passports containing contactless smart card chips that carry

Donald Davis, "E-Passports Debut, And Not Everyone Is Cheering," *Card Technology,* vol. 10, September 2005, p. 14. Copyright © 2005 SourceMedia, Inc. Reproduced by permission.

biometric data. The aim is to increase border security, but the focus may be on such issues as the privacy of personal data, whether immigration lines get longer and how much the new passports cost.

In effect, these passports would be painting giant bull's-eyes on the back of all who carry them.

Over the next decade, a half billion of the world's wealthiest consumers will be introduced to contactless smart card technology in the form of electronic passports containing contactless chips and the tiny antennas that enable those chips to transmit data over the air to passport readers.

While this opens up an important new market for contactless technology, much could go wrong. The most sensational threat is that terrorists could read data off of passports from afar and then target citizens of particular nations.

"In effect, these passports would be painting giant bull's-eyes on the back of all who carry them," the influential American Civil Liberties Union wrote this spring in a letter to the U.S. State Department. While industry executives consider such fears far-fetched, most governments will build in security measures to deter such data skimming.

But even if the passports prove secure, they could flop if they delay border crossings, forcing jet-lagged travelers to wait longer to present their passports. That fear seemed very real when early tests showed that contactless chips and readers from different vendors often did not communicate. . . .

Work on achieving interoperability between contactless chips and readers from different companies began in 2003 after the International Civil Aviation Organization, an affiliate of the United Nations that sets standards for travel documents, settled on contactless chips as the standard way electronic passports would carry data about the passport-holder.

ICAO was driven to come up with such a standard because the United States, reacting to the Sept. 11, 2001, terrorist attacks, passed a law in spring 2002 requiring friendly nations to introduce electronic passports carrying biometric data by October 2004. That deadline has since been put back twice, and now stands at October 2006. With the European Union requiring its members to introduce chip-based passports by August 2006, the new U.S. date is likely to stand.

The result is that millions of travelers will be issued passports carrying chips as their current passports expire over the next 10 years.

Exactly how many passports there are is uncertain, as no organization officially tracks them. But the consensus is that there are 500 million to 550 million passports circulating worldwide. . . .

A U.S. government study in 2002 found facial recognition accurately identified the individual only 56% of the time against a watch list of 3,000.

Biometric Identification

The point of putting chips on passports is primarily to store biometric data that can be used to verify that the person presenting the passport is the same person to whom the passport was issued. To comply with ICAO standards for electronic passports, all nations must include a digital photo on the chip, along with the textual data—name, passport number, date of issuance, and so forth—that appears on a passport's data page.

Putting that digital photo on the chip should curtail the counterfeiting of passports by criminals who substitute a photo on the data page. With an electronic passport, the border inspector would also see the photo stored on the chip when the document was issued. Changing that should be nearly impossible, since most countries will lock the chip at issuance so that no data can be added.

The digital photo can also help the inspector determine if the person standing in front of him is the passport holder when facial recognition software is applied. That software compares the image on the chip to the live image of the traveler to determine if there is a match between the two.

In such one-to-one comparisons, facial recognition has proved 98% accurate in a test Australia has been conducting with Qantas airline crew members since 2002, according to Bob Nash, head of passports in the Department of Foreign Affairs and Trade. He says human inspectors are only 60% accurate when comparing a photo to a live person. "It's not difficult to make a mistake," Nash says.

Where facial recognition does not work as well is in matching the individual against a watch list of suspected criminals or terrorists. A U.S. government study in 2002 found facial recognition accurately identified the individual only 56% of the time against a watch list of 3,000; the technology would surely fare worse against the much larger list that a major nation would compile over time.

Being able to match the person at the border against such a watch list is important because a terrorist or criminal might well obtain a passport in a false name. Fingerprints and iris scans are more accurate in one-to-many searches. That is why the European Union has mandated the addition of fingerprint data to passports three years after technical specifications are finalized, which is likely to be later [in 2005] or early 2006.

The combination of biometrics and contactless chips will make the new electronic passport far more secure than today's passports, says Barry Kefauver, a consultant and former U.S. State Department official who chairs a committee of the International Standards Organization that advises ICAO on e-passports.

"From a security integrity and facilitation point of view, the next generation of travel documents we're about to embark on is infinitely improved over the best of what we've had in the past," Kefauver says.

A Question of Convenience

Even if that proves true, travelers can lose sight of security issues if they are inconvenienced or feel their personal privacy has been compromised. For electronic passports to be viewed as a success, they will have to protect personal data, add little or no time to immigration lines, and not make it too costly to own a passport.

Privacy advocates such as the ACLU and London-based Privacy International have criticized the concept of electronic passports, saying they will lead to the creation of a global database of biometrics from millions of individuals, and hand travelers' personal data to regimes that violate human rights.

They also warn that terrorists could use the electronic passports in nefarious ways, such as using small radio frequency devices to scan a trainload of passengers coming from an airport and attacking those of a particular nationality. The ACLU proposed that passports carry a contact smart card chip to prevent such unauthorized access to passport data.

Experts in contactless technology argue that it would be difficult to skim data in real-word settings. But pressure from privacy groups has forced government agencies to take a close look at how contactless works, and in some cases led them to adopt additional security measures.

For instance, the U.S. government has changed its stance and is now "seriously considering" a technology called basic access control that Europe already has embraced. That would require a passport's data page to be opened and scanned before the chip could be read, preventing a traveler's passport from being read without their knowledge. (Sources say the

U.S. government is committed to using the technology, but will not say so publicly while it is seeking bids on passports.)

Responding to the concerns of the American Civil Liberties Union, the U.S. State Department reviewed the issue and determined that it was theoretically possible to read a contactless chip in a passport from more than 10 centimeters (just over 4 inches) away. That led the U.S. government to reconsider its position on basic access control, says Frank Moss, deputy assistant secretary for passport services.

"The ACLU has led us to take another look at our processes, and we believe we are addressing the concerns of the privacy community," Moss says. An ACLU spokesperson responds, "We're certainly glad they're taking steps to address the privacy issues and we're looking forward to seeing what exactly the details of the proposal are."

Passport officials and vendors say they have developed techniques that would thwart both of the likely forms of unauthorized access. The first is a rogue reading device powering up passport chips to surreptitiously obtain data; the second is the interception of data as it is exchanged between passport and reader.

Basic access control solves the first problem, passport officials say. Here's how it works: the border inspector scans the machine-readable data on a passport's data page. The reader uses that data to create a unique cryptographic key that is sent back to the passport chip. Only then will the chip send the personal data it contains to the reader.

Tests have shown that contactless chips can be powered up and read from more than a few inches away.

This means that the data on the chip can be accessed only by someone to whom the traveler has handed his or her passport, and not by someone carrying a hidden reader in a briefcase. Of course, someone who steals the passport also could, with an appropriate passport reader, do the same—but the thief could more easily open the book and read the information on the data page.

The protection afforded by basic access control is needed because data will not be encrypted when it is stored on the chip. The passport officials who set document standards through the International Civil Aviation Organization decided not to scramble the data for fear that some of the world's nearly 200 nations would be unable to decrypt it.

Some nations, including the United States initially, did not see the need for any protection, since the chip contains no more information than appears on the passport's data page. However, that position was based on the understanding that contactless chips could be read only from a few inches away, making it unlikely anyone would be able to read data off someone's passport without that individual being aware of it.

Contactless chips are designed to work from close range as a security feature. That way a contactless chip card used for paying transit fares, for instance, is unlikely to be read by more than one subway turnstile.

However, tests have shown that contactless chips can be powered up and read from more than a few inches away, albeit with highly sophisticated and bulky equipment.

Just how far away you can be and actually obtain data from a contactless chip is a matter of debate. Signals from a contactless chip are weak, making it hard to get an accurate read from more than a few centimeters, says Peter Kronegger, chief technology officer at ACG.

"I did some sophisticated lab experiments and found that skimming over more than 30 centimeters gets extremely tricky if not impossible," he says. Outside of a laboratory, he says, skimming from one meter away "is probably impossible."

What Are You Doing?

Even if a chip could be read from as far away as one meter, it would take a high-powered device and a large, easily noticeable antenna, says UK-based passport consultant Bill Perry.

"Somebody would get very warm standing next to that passport reader," Perry says. "The amount of energy those transmitters would have to push out to read from that type of distance would be enormous."

While this might make such snooping unlikely today, privacy advocates point out that electronic devices continually get smaller and more powerful, making it a more realistic threat in the future.

Point taken. In June, ICAO's working group on electronic passports added a recommendation that nations issuing electronic passports adopt basic access control—requiring a scan of the data page before a chip can be read. "I am not aware of any country that does not plan to go forward with basic access control," says Kefauver, the U.S. consultant.

Even if the data on a passport is secure, travelers will not be happy with their new passports if it means longer wait times.

Basic access control is "a good start," says Gus Hosein, a senior fellow at Privacy International and a visiting fellow at the London School of Economics. But he still argues for greater controls over biometric passports, including restrictions against creating massive databases with personal data.

Another early opponent of passports with contactless chips, noted U.S. computer security expert Bruce Schneier, last month reversed his opposition once he learned the U.S. would adopt basic access control.

Still in development is a system called extended access control that would add more security. It would encrypt data stored on the chip that is not already on the data page, specifically biometrics like fingerprint or iris scans.

That security system is likely to be ready by the time European nations add data from two of the individual's fingerprints to their passports as mandated by the European Union. That mandate will take effect in late 2008 or 2009, three years after specifications now being drafted are finalized, according to the UK's Carter.

The Interception Threat

The second concern about unauthorized access has to do with data being transmitted through the air between chip and reader. Basic access control is designed to thwart any evildoers by encrypting data transmitted between chip and reader, using a unique code, or key, that is created for each data-exchange session from the swipe of the passport's data page.

Even if someone were able to intercept that transmission, says Carter, "all he would get is gobbledygook."

Some nations, including the United States, may go further to make sure someone cannot stand at a distance and read data off a passport chip. They are considering adding a metal foil to the passport book that would interfere with signals from any reader that is not very close to the passport.

But Perry says this could cause problems during the production of a passport, as the issuing nation must write data to the chip and read it several times to check that the chip works. The foil could interfere with those exchanges unless it was added at the end of the production process, he says.

Even if the data on a passport is secure, travelers will not be happy with their new passports if it means longer wait times.

That prospect loomed large [in 2003] when the first tests of prototype readers found that a reader from one vendor would not necessarily read a chip from another supplier, even though both products adhered to the main contactless standard ISO 14443.

Until then, the products conforming to that ISO standard mainly were used in transit fare-collection systems. While transit operators typically mandate ISO 14443-compliant products so they can buy from many vendors, in practice the companies hired to build those transit systems would only buy from a few vendors and would tweak their products to make them work together.

But when the customers include every government on Earth, every product must work with every other product without tweaking. Otherwise, reader manufacturers would be sending their technicians out to border crossings to tune their readers to communicate with every new chip that is introduced.

There have been major "plug-tests" of chips and readers in [2005] in the United States, Australia and Japan, and each time the results have been better.

In fact, Australia's passport could be read by 15 of the 16 readers at the test in Japan in March [2005], bragged Nash, the Australian passport official, in a presentation in June at the Smart Card Summit in Sydney.

"The first day or the second day?" asks a skeptical European consultant who asked not to be named. He explains that many readers had trouble reading many chips on the first day, but that the reader manufacturers adjusted their devices to work with the passports on hand and got better results the next day.

Nash concedes in an e-mail response that some vendors had to make adjustments to read the Australian passport in the Japan trial. Nonetheless, he adds, "We do not have any lingering concerns about readers. The vendor community has embraced our requirements, and we know that there are several who can build readers that will read our passport."

One reason for his confidence is a trial that began in June [2005] in which 3,000 airline crew members from the United States, Australia and New Zealand are using electronic passports at immigration stations in airports in Los Angeles and Sydney.

"Readers in the U.S. have been reading Australian and New Zealand e-passports and readers in Australia have been reading U.S. and New Zealand e-passports," Nash says. The readers have also been able to interact with specimen passports from other countries, he says, adding, "interoperability is not an issue."

How Fast?

Even if the chips and readers work well together, the basic access control mechanism itself could lead to delays, as the chip and reader encrypt and decrypt the data they exchange. In the tests in Japan in March, it took on average 14 seconds to unlock the chip and obtain the data it contains, according to unofficial results. That could mean unwanted delays at border checkpoints.

Passport officials say the technology continues to improve. Carter says tests conducted by the United Kingdom show it takes between 3 and 8 seconds to read the data off a chip, with an average of 4 to 5 seconds. "We do not believe it will add considerable time to border-control passing."

He adds automated kiosks that make use of biometric data could speed crossings. He points to Australia, which has tested since 2002 what it calls SmartGate kiosks that identify frequent travelers using facial recognition; Australia plans this fall [2005] to introduce new kiosks that will work with the biometric data on e-passports. The United Kingdom is planning a test with automated kiosks that will use iris recognition, Carter says.

Still, some observers say the time required for the basic access control mechanism remains a serious issue. Terry Hartmann, a former Australia passport official who now is director of secure identification and biometrics for U.S.-based technology company Unisys, says 4 to 5 seconds for completing the basic access control exchange "is what they want it to be. You're looking at between 5 and 30 seconds at present."

However, Hartmann notes there is still time to improve the technology, since most countries will not deploy devices to read electronic passports until there are many such passports in the field, which will not be much before 2007. He notes new products are coming that will transmit data at 848 kilobits per second, up from 424 kbps in the current ICAO standard, although accuracy remains an issue at the higher speed.

All in all, Hartmann says, "It's definitely improving. It's better than it was a year ago [in 2004] and will be a lot better in a year's time."

How Much?

Yet another potential trouble spot for e-passports is cost. Australia raised the price of its passport by A$19 (US$14.50) to cover the new technology. The United States raised its price by $12 to $97.

Besides the cost to the citizen, privacy advocates already opposed to the e-passports are warning the projected cost of the overall programs will be even higher than governments admit. And government estimates are high. A U.S. government report has estimated it will cost $2.5 billion to roll out passports with chips and biometrics, plus $1.3 billion per year to operate the program.

The United Kingdom's program has an even higher price tag, as the government plans to also give each recipient of a passport a new national ID card in the form of a smart card, starting around 2008. The government estimates the joint card and passport program will cost £5.8 billion (US$10.2 billion) over 10 years. Much of that cost will come from the government's plans to personally interview passport applicants in order to better verify identity, rather than allow applications by mail.

But a report by the London School of Economics estimates the program could cost as much as £19 billion (US$33.4 billion). Among other things, the School of Economics doubts the passports will last 10 years, as the government says they will.

But passport officials from several countries say they believe the chip-based passports will survive the pounding of entry and exit stamps for a decade. "We've taken a view, in the end, we believe the 10-year lifetime is okay," says Bernard Herdan, chief executive of the UK Passport Service. Nash says Australia's chip supplier, Sharp Electronics of Japan, has guaranteed its chips for 12 years.

The officials note they are having their chip assemblies certified against ICAO's durability tests. But the skeptical consultant notes that no one knows if those tests will accurately forecast the durability of a passport with a chip in it. "If the tests will be sufficient," he says, "we will only find out if we have some field experience."

In short, there are several ways in which electronic passports can fall short, and critics will be ready to pounce if they do. As strange as it may seem, merely deterring terrorism may not be enough for these new passports to be deemed a success.

8

The Safety of RFID Human Implants Has Not Yet Been Established

Robert M. Sade

Robert M. Sade is a professor of surgery and director of the Institute of Human Values in Health Care at Medical University of South Carolina. He is also chair of the Council on Ethical and Judicial Affairs of the American Medical Association.

Radio-frequency identification (RFID) labeling in humans to store medical and biometric information offers promising possibilities to health care and patient safety. Nevertheless, the use of these devices is attached to not only a host of ethical issues, but possible security and physical risks. Active RFID tags, which contain internal batteries, offer benefits such as better reliability, wider transmission ranges, and increased data storage. But wider transmission ranges may threaten data security and patient privacy. Furthermore, because of their small size, RFID human implants may migrate under the skin and complicate removal. They also may interfere with the performance of electronic medical devices, such as surgical equipment and defibrillators, and medication. It is recommended that the medical community further investigate these concerns before accepting or rejecting RFID labeling in humans.

Radio frequency identification (RFID) tags are computer chips connected to miniature antennae that can be used to transmit information electronically via a proximate RFID reader. The use of these devices in health care represents another promising development in information technology, but also raises important ethical, legal and social issues. Specifically, the use of RFID labeling in humans for medical purposes may improve patient safety, but also may pose some physical risks, compromise patient privacy, or present other social hazards. . . .

Background

Radio frequency identification devices utilize wireless technology to communicate data via signals in the radio frequency range of the electromagnetic spectrum. Data are stored in a microchip attached to an antenna, and packaged so that they can be attached to or embedded in products, animals, or people.

The two main types of RFID tags are passive and active. Passive tags contain no internal power supply. They convert the radio frequency energy emitted from a reader device into signals that transmit stored data for a distance of a few feet. These passive devices currently have restricted amounts of data storage and are of limited functionality, because the information they contain cannot be modified.

In comparison, active RFID tags contain an internal battery, which provides increased reliability, longer transmission ranges, on-tag data processing and greater data storage. While their capacity to process data internally allows for expanded capabilities in the future, their greater transmission range presents a more substantial threat to data confidentiality and patients' privacy.

In October 2004, the U.S. Food and Drug Administration (FDA) approved the first RFID tags specifically intended for human implantation. Approved RFID devices are currently limited to passive units, intended for identifying patients. Active RFID chips may be approved in the future.

Human-implanted passive RFID devices that identify patients may also contain essential biometric and medical information. The tags are primarily intended for patients with chronic diseases, such as coronary artery disease, chronic obstructive pulmonary disease, diabetes mellitus, stroke or seizure disorder, or are implanted into patients with medical devices such as pacemakers, stents, or joint replacements. These devices are approximately the size of a grain of rice, and are implanted under the skin via a hypodermic-type needle in less than one minute.

Information Systems

RFID tags may promote the timely identification of patients and expedite access to their medical information. As a result, these devices can improve the continuity and coordination of care with resulting reduction in adverse drug events and other medical errors.

RFID tags also may improve efficiency within the health care system. In conjunction with improved medical record management, these devices may facilitate access to patient records, medication lists, and diagnostic tests. To be maximally effective, however, the information in these devices must be adequately integrated into present clinical information and communications systems, laboratory databases, and pharmacy systems.

Appropriate processes also must be developed to inscribe, read and archive data stored on RFID tags. As new designs enter the marketplace, the emergence of competing standards may present problems for hospital staff if a patient's ID tag proves incompatible with the interrogation devices employed by the hospital.

Physical Risks to Patients

These devices may present physical risks to the patient. Though they are removable, their small size allows them to migrate under the skin, making them potentially difficult to extract. However, this tendency may be minimized by constructing RFID tags from materials that permit surrounding tissue to encase the device. In addition, RFID tags may cause electromagnetic interference, which may interfere with electrosurgical devices and defibrillators. Finally, it has not been determined whether RFID tags might affect the efficacy of pharmaceuticals.

The medical profession must continue to monitor the efficacy of [RFID].

Patient Privacy and Security

The primary concerns surrounding human RFID labeling pertain to their potential impact on patient privacy and security. Physicians must assure patients that their medical information will be held in confidence. Moreover, maintenance of privacy is required to protect patients from embarrassment, potential social discrimination, loss of health care coverage, or other detrimental consequences.

At this time, the security of RFID devices has not been fully established. Physicians, therefore, cannot assure patients that the personal information contained on RFID tags will be appropriately protected. In light of these security concerns, the FDA currently requires RFID transponders to store only a unique electronic identification code to be read by the scanner. This identification code can then be used to access patient identity and corresponding health information stored in a database.

To protect confidentiality and privacy, the medical community should advocate for the adoption of other protections, such as computer encryption or digital signatures. Ultimately, the medical community should undertake appropriate efforts to prevent unauthorized access to patients' information contained on RFID tags.

Informed Consent

To properly respect patient autonomy, RFID tags should not be implanted or removed without the prior consent of patients or their surrogates. During the consent process, decision-makers should be informed of the potential risks and benefits associated with RFID tags, including the many uncertainties regarding their efficacy. Patients are also entitled to know who will be granted access to the data contained on RFID tags and the purposes for which this information will be used.

Further Considerations

It seems likely that utilization of RFID devices for medical purposes will expand. The medical profession must continue to monitor the efficacy of these devices. If RFID tags are proven to benefit patient care significantly, the profession should advocate for widespread adoption of RFID technology, and for policies that make RFID tags available to all patients who would benefit.

However, if objective evidence demonstrates negative consequences that outweigh the benefits in relation to health care, the medical profession will bear an important responsibility to oppose the use of RFID labeling in humans.

Finally, physicians should be aware of emerging non-medical applications of human-implantable RFID devices. For instance, active RFID technologies might be considered for the tracking or surveillance of individuals who pose a threat to others. Although this is only one of many possible uses of RFID technology in the future, it alerts the medical profession to the need for continuous assessment of the appropriate role of physicians participating in RFID labeling of human beings.

Indeed, certain uses could constitute an infringement upon patients' individual liberties, placing physicians in a position to act as patient advocates by promoting the use of other, less intrusive alternatives, when available.

RFID technology has the potential to improve patient care as well as patient safety. However, the safety and efficacy of human-implantable RFID devices has yet to be established. Therefore, the medical community should support further investigations to obtain the data necessary to make informed medical decisions regarding the use of these devices. The medical community should also be sensitive to potential social consequences of RFID devices, such as non-medical applications in law enforcement.

9

RFID Human Implants May Not Be Ethical

Kenneth R. Foster and Jan Jaeger

Kenneth R. Foster is a bioengineering professor at the University of Pennsylvania in Philadelphia and fellow at the Institute of Electrical and Electronics Engineers. Jan Jaeger is a former emergency room nurse and teaches at the University of Pennsylvania's School of Nursing.

Radio-frequency identification (RFID) implants for medical purposes would be beneficial to patients with Alzheimer's, certain mental illnesses, and other special needs. But their use among the general population could open the door to unethical chipping practices. Some companies encourage or require employees to be implanted with RFID, and several government officials have discussed chipping guest workers in the United States. These scenarios depict the unethical use of RFID human implants, blurring the line between "voluntary" and coerced implantation and eroding bodily rights. Other harms include the dangers to privacy and the risk of identity theft. The alternative to human RFID implants, biometric scanners, are less ethically suspect and may be the ultimate solution.

Wanted: Power-systems engineer with experience in high-power (5–100-kW) motor-controller design. Must be U.S. citizen and have valid ISO1443-compatible access-control RFID implant.

Kenneth R. Foster and Jan Jaeger, "RFID Inside," *IEEE Spectrum*, March 2007, http://www.spectrum.ieee.org. Copyright © 2007 IEEE. Reproduced by permission of the publisher and author.

Sound farfetched? Today, yes. A decade from now, maybe not.

With the proliferation of radio-frequency identification technology and the recent, but increasing, use of implantable RFID chips in humans, we may already be on a path that would make such an ad commonplace in a 2017 issue of *IEEE Spectrum.*

The benefits would be undeniable—an implantable RFID chip, which is durable and about the size of a grain of rice, can hold or link to information about the identity, physiological characteristics, health, nationality, and security clearances of the person it's embedded in. The proximity of your hand could start your car or unlock your front door or let an emergency room physician know you are a diabetic even if you are unconscious. Once implanted, the chip and the information it contains are always with you—you'd never lose your keys again.

Do you really want to be required to have a foreign object implanted in your arm just to get or keep a job?

A Darker Side

But there is a darker side, namely the erosion of our privacy and our right to bodily integrity. After all, do you really want to be required to have a foreign object implanted in your arm just to get or keep a job? And once you have it, do you really want your employer to know whenever you leave the office? And do you want every RFID reader-equipped supermarket checkout counter to note your presence and your purchases?

Until a couple of years ago, chipping humans was largely the domain of cybernetics provocateurs like Kevin Warwick or hobbyists like Amal Graafstra. . . . Then, in 2004, the U.S. Food and Drug Administration, which regulates medical devices in the United States, approved an RFID tag for implantation in humans as a means of accessing a person's health records.

This tag, called VeriChip, is a short-range transponder that relies on the signal from a reader unit for its power supply.

When exposed to a varying magnetic field from the reader, the chip powers itself up and repeatedly transmits a 16-digit code that is unique to the tag. According to the company, 2000 people have already had tags implanted.

The VeriChip tag is part of a health information system called VeriMed. The code contained in the implanted chip points to a record in a database identifying the patient and containing that patient's health records. By scanning a person's chip, caregivers can retrieve an identification code that enables them to access the medical history of people who cannot otherwise communicate their identities—speeding up their treatment and possibly saving their lives.

VeriChip Corp., a subsidiary of Applied Digital Solutions, headquartered in Delray, Fla., is also promoting its device as a security measure. It has six clients around the world, five of which use the implant as a secondary source of authentication, says Keith Bolton, vice president of government and international affairs for VeriChip. The highest-profile example of this application came in 2004 when the attorney general of Mexico and 18 of his staff had chips implanted to allow them to gain access to certain high-security areas.

The tag is also finding use as a kind of implanted credit card. In trendy nightclubs in the Netherlands, Scotland, Spain, and the United States, patrons can get "chipped"—at a cost of about US $165 in one establishment. In future visits, "by the time you walk through the door to the bar," one proprietor told Britain's *Daily Telegraph*, "your favorite drink is waiting for you, and the bar staff can greet you by name."

And the list of proposed applications could grow quickly. VeriChip is advancing a scheme to "chip" soldiers, as a replacement for a soldier's traditional dog tag, and a VeriChip officer has proposed chipping guest workers entering the United States.

VeriChip Corp.'s well-meaning attempt to improve personal health care may serve as a beachhead to wider use.

The Real Dangers

Before too many of those suggestions become realities, we need to examine carefully the very real dangers that RFID implants could pose to our privacy and our freedom. If we don't figure out the risks and come up with ways to mitigate them, someone answering that ad for a power engineer may live in a world with considerably less privacy and feel compelled to have an implant just to be able to get a job.

The VeriChip tag's main use, as a means of identifying patients who might be unable to communicate with caregivers and of accessing their medical records, could clearly be lifesaving in emergency situations. As long as the patient has provided informed consent and the privacy of the patient's medical records is adequately protected, there are few ethical concerns with the technology. But VeriChip Corp.'s well-meaning attempt to improve personal health care may serve as a beachhead for wider use, and that expansion could create urgent ethical issues, particularly if an element of coercion enters into the process.

Consider, for example, a proposal by Scott Silverman, CEO of VeriChip. In an interview on 16 May 2006 on Fox News Channel (a U.S. television network), he proposed implanting chips in immigrants and guest workers to assist the government in later identifying them. Shortly afterward, the Associated Press quoted President Álvaro Uribe of Colombia as telling a U.S. senator that he would agree to require Colombian citizens to be implanted with RFID chips before they could gain entry into the United States for seasonal work.

Guest workers might ostensibly consent to having chips implanted. But would chipping them be truly voluntary? Such "voluntary" actions may determine a person's ability to earn a living, and the worker might not view the implantation as something he or she could refuse. What person facing poverty at home and given the prospect of a job in a different country would be in a position to argue?

At a practical level, when chips are implanted in guest laborers, who pays for the cost of purchasing, implanting, and monitoring the chips in hundreds or thousands of poor migrants? If someone has an adverse reaction to the chip so that it has to be removed or replaced, who bears that cost? And who pays if the chips become obsolete or compromised by rampant cloning—the illicit duplication of the supposedly unique device—and have to be replaced? Affluent patrons of a trendy club might gladly pay to be chipped, but the situation would certainly be different for those pursuing temporary minimum-wage jobs in a foreign country.

Silverman made his proposal, that immigrants and guest workers be implanted with RFID chips, amid a national debate in the United States about illegal immigration, focusing on impoverished Latin Americans in search of work. But might Silverman's proposition apply as well to electrical engineers or doctors, or other high-status individuals coming into the country for work? Who decides?

Mandating guest workers to have RFID chips implanted in their bodies for identification purposes strikes us as coercive and opportunistic. That approach makes the RFID chip a branding device similar to what a cowboy uses when he sears the haunches of his cattle or the tattoos that the Nazis forced on their victims in concentration camps. It goes against the widely held belief in basic human rights and might even be interpreted as a violation of Article 3 of the United Nations'

Universal Declaration of Human Rights, which affirms everybody's right to "life, liberty, and security of person."

Social researchers are just beginning to study people's attitudes to implanted RFID. Christine Perakslis and Robert Wolk at Bridgewater State University, in Massachusetts, questioned 141 college students on their feelings about implanted RFID. Respondents were asked if they would be willing to have an implant to prevent ID theft, to combat terrorism, for other national security reasons, as a life-saving device, or to ensure the safety of themselves and their families. About a third of the respondents were willing to be implanted, while less than half of them were not. Wolk and Perakslis's subjects were the least comfortable with chipping as a cure for ID theft. The reasons that garnered the most support for getting chipped were to save their lives or to ensure the safety of their family.

Another small survey in 2003 by Starr Roxanne Hiltz, professor of information systems at the New Jersey Institute of Technology, in Newark, and her colleagues found that 18 out of 23 people questioned objected to the idea of implantable chips as identification.

Changing Yourself

Some of the resistance has to do with feelings about modification to one's body. "If they are putting something inside of you," one respondent replied, "it's like you're changing yourself. It's not right." As the wide variety of acceptable and unacceptable piercings and tattoos found around the world attests, people of different backgrounds vary in their attitudes toward "changing yourself."

Tattoos, an ID technology that is at least 4000 years old, share some key qualities with implanted RFID tags. Both could be used for the same purposes and are intended to be permanent—they can be removed, but only with some difficulty and not without assistance. The only differences are that, compared with a tattoo, an RFID chip is invisible, may be easier to read surreptitiously, and is a little more difficult to duplicate. Yet we suspect most people, regardless of their feelings toward being chipped, would balk at the idea of accepting a machine-readable tattoo as a means of identification, even if such an indelible marking had some personal or societal benefit.

There is no clear medical or business justification for chipping large populations of healthy people.

If there were a societal benefit, could a government require individuals to modify their bodies? For public health purposes, the answer is yes. In the United States, for example, students must have certain immunizations before attending public school. But this example is the only instance we can think of. Could a health care-related implant such as the VeriChip tag become a public health imperative? Would that use lead down a slippery slope toward universal chipping? It seems unlikely.

VeriChip Corp. does not, in fact, advocate universal chipping for medical purposes. The company's vice president of medical applications, Richard Seelig, estimates a U.S. market for VeriMed of 43 million to 45 million people—less than one-sixth of the population. This group is made up of people who are more likely than others to wind up in the emergency room. These include cancer patients undergoing chemotherapy; people with pacemakers or other medical implants; and those who might be suffering some sort of cognitive impairment or loss of consciousness due to epilepsy, diabetes, or Alzheimer's disease.

We believe that even Seelig's estimates of the potential size of the market for patient identification are grossly exaggerated. "For certain subpopulations—Alzheimer's patients, the mentally ill, people with communication difficulties—having an implanted identifier makes great sense," says John Halamka, a former emergency physician and now CIO at Beth Israel

Deaconess Medical Center, in Boston. "Others can just carry a card in their wallet, a medic-alert bracelet, or a USB drive with their personal health records. There is no clear medical or business justification for chipping large populations of healthy people."

In fact, so far there is no clear evidence that the VeriChip will help patients facing medical emergencies. The first study designed to determine whether patients, physicians, and insurers benefit at all from VeriChip began only last fall, in New Jersey.

Other nonimplanted technologies based on RFIDs may soon provide some of the benefits to the patient VeriChip hopes for. For instance, nonprofit health care informatics organization MedicAlert is researching RFID-enabled bracelets that would link to a personal health care record. However, as with VeriChip, a key question is how to ensure the privacy of the information in the databases, while at the same time providing easy access to the database by caregivers in emergency situations.

Privacy Is at the Heart

A right to privacy is at the heart of some of the questions raised by implanted RFID tags. In agreeing to be chipped for medical purposes, the patient gives up a measure of privacy for his or her own potential benefit. But when chipping is used for other reasons, difficult confidentiality issues can arise. When a business gives an identity card to a newly hired worker, for example, the company retains ownership of the card. But will the employer also own the chip inside an employee's body?

A test case may be on the horizon: the first U.S. company to implant employees with VeriChip, CityWatcher.com, in Cincinnati, recently closed its doors. Its CEO, Sean Darks, himself an implantee, did not return repeated phone calls inquiring whether employees kept their implants after the company folded. VeriChip itself makes no recommendation about whether former employees should be "dechipped," says the company's Bolton. But he says removal is a quick and easy procedure. "I've had many [chips] in and out of my body," he says. Perhaps just as important a question as who owns the chip is that of who owns the data on the chip. Can the tag be read and its data used without the consent of the person who has it implanted?

Fears that some individuals have expressed about being tracked through an implanted chip are probably unrealistic. The VeriChip and most other passive RFID devices, those that derive their power from the reader, provide only an identification number and can be probed only from very short distances. The VeriChip is readable only at 10 centimeters or less using its handheld scanner.

This distance can be increased, however, using more efficient antennas. Digital Angel Corp., in St. Paul, Minn., also owned by VeriChip's parent company, Applied Digital Solutions, is developing a "walk-through" scanner with greater range. Nevertheless, the prospects of a "drive-by" theft of a person's identity seem remote, and even more remote is the possibility that the government or some other organization might track an individual moving about in ordinary life.

Still, if the computer age has one lesson, it is that systems and data are invariably less secure than their proponents claim. Particularly troubling for a device that is being marketed for access control, the VeriChip lacks modern cryptographic and other protections and is prey to simple attacks. In a recently published article in the *Journal of the American Medical Informatics Association*, Beth Israel's Halamka and colleagues showed how easily a simple-to-build device can scan the chip and replay the radio signal to fool a VeriChip reader.

This flaw may be insignificant when the chip is being used for identification purposes—for example, with an Alzheimer's patient. But Halamka and his coauthors argue forcefully that the chip should not be used for authentication purposes to control access to sensitive areas or information.

Though for now they store nothing more than a number, inevitably, implanted RFID chips will store more data and databases will be created that link information on implanted chips to other facts about a person. It is easy to foresee situations in which even a simple identification number might lead to harm—consider the millions of dollars lost to identity theft in the United States because of the disclosure of Social Security numbers and similar data.

We have all already been issued our fingerprints.

What Can We Do?

So what can we do about implanted RFID's impending problems? Using legislation to restrict their use is an obvious measure; in fact, laws are already in the works. Faced with widespread public concerns about this technology, more than 10 U.S. states have enacted laws limiting implants. In May 2006, for example, Wisconsin passed a bill that would prohibit requiring anybody to have a microchip implanted.

But laws might be difficult to enforce if implanted chips, like drivers' licenses, remain voluntary but become de facto requirements for many kinds of employment or services. And the Wisconsin law does nothing to allay worries about the loss of privacy. Governments may need to make the unauthorized reading of an implanted RFID tag illegal as well.

Some of the ethical concerns can be addressed with better technology. Ari Juels, head of RSA Laboratories, the R&D arm of RSA Security, in Bedford, Mass., believes that, with proper encryption methods, a person's privacy can be preserved without decreasing the usefulness of the implant. Juels says that the ease with which a thief can steal a VeriChip radio signal makes the tag a poor security tool, but that it eliminates a thief's incentive to kidnap or carve someone up. So together with Halamka and others, he developed a technique that still lets a thief copy the chip's radio signal but at the same time keeps the actual ID number it represents safe. Lest you think criminals would not go to such extremes, in 2005 BBC News reported that thieves stole a car protected by a fingerprint-reading lock by chopping off the owner's finger.

Halamka's solution, by the way, would make it impossible to track an implanted individual by noting which RFID readers—at stores, doors, gas pumps—picked up his or her radio signature. Crucial to Juels's technology is that the chip's radio signature changes unpredictably each time it's read, even though the bits it encodes remain the same.

But maybe the ultimate solution, to allow accurate identification of individuals without some of the ethical issues raised by implanted radio chips, might require a different technology completely—biometric scanners. Although such devices are more costly than RFID-chip readers, they will inevitably become more affordable with time. And the "tags" are always going to be more competitive: after all, we have all already been issued our fingerprints.

10

RFID Technology Can Benefit the Supply Chain Significantly

AME Info

Based in the United Arab Emirates, AME Info is an online provider of business news and information for the Middle East.

The adoption of radio-frequency identification (RFID) will optimize the supply chain—the complex, organized web of people and technologies that moves products and services from supplier to consumer—and benefit many industries. Retail giant Wal-Mart, an early adopter of RFID, saves billions of dollars annually using the technology to avoid out-of-stock inventory, prevent theft and fraud, and enhance tracking of their shipments. RFID systems also promise to help companies cut costs, improve their products, and increase sales. There are still obstacles to implementing RFID—the current high price of the tags makes it impractical to use for numerous products, and technology standards have not yet been achieved. But RFID is here to stay, and its value in enterprise will grow.

Squeezing cost and inefficiency out of the supply chain has been one of the recurring mantras of the industrialised world for the past 50 years.

The concept, as we would recognise it, has its roots in the Toyota Production System (TPS) of the 1950s and has been refined and improved significantly over the years to the point where one might expect that the most sophisticated devotees today have optimised their supply chains.

AME Info, "How RFID Can Help Optimise Supply Chain Management," AME Info, August 21, 2005. http://ameinfo.com. Reproduced by permission.

The journey towards perfection, however, never ends. In the very near future, the adoption of sensor-based Radio Frequency Identification (RFID) technology will allow the creation of the real-time, sensor-connected manufacturing plant. By adding RFID tags to every product, tool, resource and item of materials handling equipment, manufacturers will be able to get better demand signals from customers and the market.

At its core, RFID is simply an enabling technology that has the potential of helping retailers provide the right product at the right place at the right time, thus maximising sales and profits. RFID provides the technology to identify uniquely each container, pallet, case and item being manufactured, shipped and sold, thus providing the building blocks for increased visibility throughout the supply chain.

The technology will bring benefits to a wide range of industries, as we shall see, but one of the main drivers of RFID adoption has been the retail sector, led by Wal-Mart in the U.S. Phillip J. Windley, an Associate Professor of Computer Science at Brigham Young University, estimates that U.S. retail giant Wal-Mart alone could save $8.35 billion annually with RFID—that's more than the total revenue of half the companies in the Fortune 500.

His massive total is made up as follows: $600 million through avoiding stock-outs; $575 million by avoiding theft, error and vendor fraud; $300 million through better tracking of a billion pallets and cases; $180 million through reduced inventory; and a huge $6.7 billion by eliminating the need to have people scan barcodes in the supply chain and in-store. Small wonder, then, that Wal-Mart is investing $3 billion in RFID over several years and is one of the leading proponents of RFID implementation.

How It Works

RFID is a system of small electronic tags (comprising a tiny chip plus an antenna) that transmit data via a radio signal to

RFID readers and related hardware and software infrastructure. The transmitters can be placed anywhere that tracking the movement of goods adds value to the commercial process: on containers, pallets, materials handling equipment, cases or even on individual products.

The information on tags is read when they pass by an RFID reader, and that movement is captured and managed by the infrastructure. In this way, organisations are able to link the physical world to the digital world without any human interaction. Whatever actions are then triggered depends on the individual application, from basic stock replenishment at one end of the spectrum to facilitating the ultimate lean supply chain at the other.

A New Era

RFID promises to revolutionise supply chains and usher in a new era of cost savings, efficiency and business intelligence. The potential applications are vast as it is relevant to any organisation engaged in the production, movement or sale of physical goods. This includes retailers, distributors, logistics service providers, manufacturers and their entire supplier base, hospitals and pharmaceuticals companies, and the entire food chain.

It has the potential to improve efficiency and visibility, cut costs, deliver better asset utilisation, produce higher quality goods, reduce shrinkage and counterfeiting, and increase sales by reducing out-of-stocks. It can even help improve the safety of the food and pharmaceuticals we buy.

The key to delivering all these benefits is cost. The falling price of RFID tags is a driver for the technology. One Canadian consumer products manufacturer has established that RFID becomes revenue-neutral at 15 cents per tag, at which point the prospect of RFID as a replacement for barcode labels becomes very real indeed.

Tag pricing is critical. Industry is hoping that tag manufacturers can hit 5 cents per unit, and that is being regarded as a breakthrough level. Yet even that is still too expensive for, say, an individual can of Coke, which is why packaging companies and other researchers are looking at innovative ways to apply this technology. In the coming years, at least, we are likely to see RFID tags and barcodes existing side by side.

The path to RFID nirvana is not without its obstacles: tag costs are still high; readers can't always read all the cases on a pallet; one frequency and one tag design does not fit all; standards are in a state of flux; end-users lack real RFID knowledge; and radio interference can upset the best-laid plans. Wal-Mart laid down its marker as an RFID pioneer by issuing mandates to its suppliers throughout the entire supply chain. Wal-Mart, Metro Group, Tesco, Target and the U.S. Department of Defense all told their top suppliers to incorporate RFID tags in all pallet shipments by 2005. Wal-Mart then relented a little, having found that not only would its suppliers find the deadline hard to meet, but so would Wal-Mart itself. Wal-Mart is now on track to have RFID in 600 stores and 12 distribution centres by the end of [2005]. . . .

Winners All Around

Whether it enters the mainstream this year or next or even in 2010, the business value of RFID is undeniable. It will create winners all round. Manufacturers will benefit from increased inventory visibility, more efficient use of labour, better line operations and improved fulfilment. Retailers can benefit from reduced inventory, because the improved supply chain visibility allows better demand forecasting, lower safety stocks and lower order cycle times. Automated data capture will also cut costs by reducing labour in the store and warehouse, and fewer sales will be lost through out-of-stocks.

And it's not just the retail sector that will benefit. Manufacturing industry as a whole will be able to fine-tune the supply chain to optimise efficiency and minimise inventory and waste. RFID tags in car sub-assemblies will make safety checks and recalls faster and easier. Tags in sub-sea structures like oil and gas pipelines will make maintenance and repair simpler. Hospitals will be able to maximise their return on assets by tracking the whereabouts of expensive and life-saving equipment at all times.

The pharmaceutical industry will be able to reduce or even eliminate counterfeiting by giving each unit of dosage a unique Electronic Product Code (EPC) number. This will allow data to be recorded and be accessible to all supply chain partners on a drug's current location, all historical locations, the time spent at each location and environmental storage conditions throughout its life.

There is no doubt that RFID and other sensor-based technologies present massive potential for creating competitive advantage.

The technology will benefit lots of other industries, too. Customer returns will be facilitated for the consumer electronics sector; aerospace will have safer handling of hazardous materials; port security will be improved; the logistics and transportation industry will have better management of truck yards, container yards, shipping yards and cross-docking activity; consumer packaged goods will have easier receiving reconciliation, better lot tracking, faster and less expensive product recall and all the benefits associated with improved visibility throughout the supply chain.

RFID is best viewed as part of a broader spectrum of sensor-based technologies. This includes the now-familiar technologies of barcode and magnetic stripe, as well as integration with equipment such as scales and dimensioning devices and sensors for such things as temperature, position and moisture. Hybrid sensors that combine RFID tags with temperature sensors, all embedded in a barcode label, are already available.

Multiple point solutions aimed at each sensor-based niche simply will not scale and will not provide the best return on investment. As a result, any RFID capability must be part of a comprehensive technology and applications infrastructure that can collect events from these disparate sources, combine the data into composite transactions and then automatically trigger the appropriate business process.

There is no doubt that RFID and other sensor-based technologies present massive potential for creating competitive advantage. Companies in these and other industries will find that incorporating these technologies into their information infrastructure and integrating them into their business processes will provide substantial business benefit. But, to realise maximum return on investment, they need to leverage their information architecture strategically.

If RFID is to create value for business, first it will create data—masses of data. Users will need to ensure they have an IT architecture that can appropriately manage, analyse and respond to this new wealth of data being captured to truly gain visibility into their supply chain. . . .

RFID Is Here to Stay

Two things are crystal clear: RFID is here to stay, and enterprises can achieve significant business value from embracing it. Due to the high cost of investing in RFID, each company needs to evaluate its own business processes to determine where and if RFID can be applied to improve operational and process efficiencies to positively affect the bottom line. . . .

The early adopters are already well down the road towards RFID. At the very least, now is a great time for all businesses to start developing their own RFID strategy.

11

RFID Technology's Benefits for the Supply Chain May Be Exaggerated

Ronan Clinton

Ronan Clinton is managing director of Heavey RF, a radio-frequency technology company based in Dublin, Ireland.

Radio-frequency identification (RFID) is hyped as the cutting-edge successor to the bar code and the magic solution to the logistical challenges of the supply chain, the network of personnel and technology that suppliers use to deliver products and services to consumers. While it does have its technological merits, RFID cannot live up to the aforementioned hype. Bar codes are simply much more cost effective and not hampered by the technical restrictions of RFID, primarily the necessity for hundreds of different tags for different products, which may or may not work. Thus, companies from smaller countries are recommended to hold off on implementing RFID technology for their supply chains, as they are not likely to realize the benefits gained by their larger international counterparts.

Before I start, I would like to categorically state that I am a very big fan of RFID. Since 1995, I have been exposed to various methods of solving unique problems using RFID and I have been directly involved in RFID projects. [Radio-frequency technology company] Heavey RF has a large range of RFID products to offer and has deployed RFID solutions to a number of companies in Ireland. Unlike most RFID providers, we have actually made money doing it.

Ronan Clinton, "RFID Bomb?" HeaveyRF.com, July 20, 2007. Copyright © 2008 Heavey RF.com. Reproduced by permission.

Not a Magic Wand

So what's the problem?

The problem is this—RFID simply cannot do what people expect it to do from the hype that has been generated over the last decade. It is not a magic wand that will tell you where all your products are in real time. It is not as reliable as bar coding, and can never be as cost effective. While mankind frequently bends the laws of physics, we have never actually broken them, which is what would have to be done if the technology were to be able to live up to the hype.

I do not envisage that RFID will die a death—far from it, but I do argue that it will never replace the bar code.

RFID describes a multitude of devices and components, but is generally understood as a technology that uses computer chips to store information. The beauty is that a lot of RFID chips or tags do not need power as they are charged by the emitted reading signal and respond according to the data programmed therein. The benefit in modern industry over conventional methods of tracking items, such as bar coding, is that comparatively large volumes of data can be stored in a tag and line of sight is not necessarily required. The technology is being sold globally as a revolution that will eventually replace bar codes. The hype is that if you are not on board, you will be left behind. Sound familiar? Remember the dot com industry in the late 1990s?

I compare RFID to the dot com industry because of the similarities that can be drawn between the two. RFID technology has been around a long time, as was the internet before general adoption. Then, a huge perceived explosion in the dot com industry was generated around speculation, hype and a fear of not being part of a "new economy"—a phase that RFID is currently in. When the dust settled and reality played its part, the dot com industry began a more sustainable and organic development—the next phase for RFID. I do not envisage that RFID will die a death—far from it, but I do argue that it will never replace the bar code, and I also argue that it will never reach a level where all the products we buy in a "supermarket of the future" are electronically tagged. It just isn't viable, and never can be.

If you are an Irish company who does not have an RFID strategy, you have absolutely nothing to worry about. If it is ever legislated or mandated to you that you must have RFID in place in your company, you are actually better off waiting as long as possible to reap the benefits of the ongoing developments. (No RFID discussion is complete without discussing Wal-Mart's mandate, and this paper is no different—more on that later. . .). Now is not the time to be developing strategies. Now is the time to learn about RFID, what it is, what it can do and more importantly what it can't do. Only then can you make informed decisions about even having a strategy.

You cannot guarantee that all your current and future products will work with a particular type of tag.

Barriers to Success

There are two core reasons why RFID will not succeed in replacing barcode technology—technical restrictions and cost. As I type, I can almost hear the advocators saying—"cost is constantly coming down and will eventually be affordable" and "all technical difficulties can be overcome." The old story about the Russians using a pencil in space springs to mind. Bar codes are more reliable than RFID tags—a fact that if you do some basic research will turn up some surprising reading. (Some reports have read rates of UHF Gen II tags as low as 60% success at case level.)

RFID tags will never be as cost effective as bar codes. Ever. I state this in the same way that a helicopter will never be as cost effective as a motorcar. Sound bizarre? Think about it. The RFID advocators will tell you that bulk purchases will drive the cost of the tag downwards. That is like a helicopter manufacturer telling you that if everybody buys helicopters, the cost will come down to the cost of a car, and when that happens, you would want to have a helicopter because they have less boundaries, a better view and get you from A to B quicker. I do not want to get bogged down in the complexities of global helicopter adoption—I am merely making a point.

The auto ID industry set a benchmark a number of years ago that when RFID tags reached 5 cents, general adoption would be possible. I believe that the 5-cent tag in a useable form will never be possible. The 5-cent tag has been predicted based on the massive volumes that would be involved should global adoption take place. However, the big problem here is that there is no "one size fits all," a factor needed to drive the volumes. In reality, there are hundreds of different RFID tag types. From short range, medium range, long range, LF, HF, UHY, 2.4GHz, 5GHz—all with different physical attributes depending on the product they are to be applied to. Because of the physical size of products (from very small to very large), their contents (foodstuffs containing iron or viscous materials), and the properties of RF technology, a large number of different tag types need to be maintained—splitting volumes. In the supply chain, RFID could only ever be effective if 100% readability was possible, which it isn't. Anyone who tells you different doesn't understand the technology. You cannot guarantee that all your current and future products will work with a particular type of tag.

In the USA, debates are still raging about which technology to use. Wal-Mart has stipulated a UHF tag, and other large pharmaceutical manufacturers have gone down a HF path, as it is better suited to their requirements. Now what happens if a company who was mandated by Wal-Mart to have a UHF tag suddenly receives a mandate from another company to have a HF tag? Everything has to be reinvented. Any barcode scanner worth its salt can read a whole range of barcode symbologies. Having two different tag frequencies from a reading perspective is like trying to listen to two radio stations at the same time—try it and you will see that you will not be able to understand either.

RFID has many fantastic uses. I personally have two RFID tags on my key-ring and one in my wallet in the form of access control and the central locking for my car. They work, rarely let me down and I'm happy. Looking at the cost (€15 for my access control tag and a recent fee of €193 for my car key when my remote central locking actually stopped working) I would like to make the point that all three RFID tags I carry with me daily are completely different in terms of size, readability, radio frequency, data and proximity. This is because they are fit for purpose—I don't want to have to be within 1 inch of my car to be able to open it, and I don't want my access control cards opening doors from 50 feet away.

I have attended seminar after seminar over the last number of years, listening to the same lectures about how RFID is the future and that if you are not on board you will be left behind. I have not heard anything new in these seminars and most of them seem to focus on the biggest thing to happen to RFID in the last 10 years—Wal-Mart.

A Very Different Picture

When your biggest customer says 'jump,' you say 'how high.' When Wal-Mart issued a mandate in 2003 to their top 100 suppliers to have RFID tags in place on their cases and pallet deliveries by January 1, 2005, RFID was put in the spotlight because the suppliers had no real choice. Indeed, these were exciting times—if this worked, then a global acceptance would surely follow and speculation of a technology revolution of gargantuan proportions was upon us.

Speculation involves taking a risk against the possibility of dramatic, astounding success. The Wal-Mart story has made RFID look like a sure thing. However, speculation is at its riskiest when it looks like a sure thing. Scratch the surface of the Wal-Mart progress and a very different picture to the reported successes emerges. The *Wall Street Journal* wrote a piece about how RFID in Wal-Mart was failing, which was quickly disputed by Wal-Mart, but no real defence was produced in terms of facts or figures or indeed the much sought after return on investment.

On paper, the numbers may add up for Wal-Mart (after all, they are not paying for most of it. . .), but suppliers are not seeing a return on investment. Some are more outspoken than others, but hey, are you going to criticize your biggest customer in public? To date, not one of the Wal-Mart suppliers utilizes RFID for any other customer. There is also the danger that other customers issue different mandates with different non-compatible requirements and the RFID headache gets twice as bad for many suppliers.

RFID technology in 95% of cases presented to me would be technology for technology's sake.

Irish companies are being advised by systems integrators and standards bodies to implement RFID now to avoid being left behind. I would advise Irish companies to hold off implementing RFID unless it can be demonstrated that it is fit for purpose and a return of investment can be obtained by the carefully planned change of processes. Why implement RFID for the sake of it? If a company is issued a mandate to have RFID on products, then this can be implemented at the back door without huge costs of implementing RFID throughout an operation. Irish companies and industries are comparatively small on a global stage and as such will always find difficulty realizing benefits that have been identified in the supply chain in larger countries. For example, there is a proven use of RFID in large bulk storage warehouses with no racking. However, when I explored the possibility of implementing such a solution in one of the largest bulk storage warehouses in Ireland, it never got off the ground as the scale of the operation was just not big enough to warrant it.

A Big Leap of Faith

Why do I feel the need to write this? Because I actually believe in RFID as part of Heavey RF's future. I have predicted that as much as 20% of Heavey RF's business could be RFID related over the next 5-year period complementary to our existing bar code and voice-directed work. We have some extremely advanced RFID products and software and some very innovative ideas where we can offer productivity, accuracy and competitive advantages. However, the bigger the hype that is generated, the more sour the taste in the mouths of would-be customers at the mere mention of RFID in the future. I want people to understand that RFID has a place in Irish industry, but a very different place to what is currently being portrayed.

RFID technology in 95% of cases presented to me would be technology for technology's sake. I have had customers question why I have not brought this ground breaking technology instead of bar coding to them to reduce costs and improve accuracy only to scratch the surface and be thanked by them afterwards for saving them from a big mistake. RFID can produce some real benefits when deployed correctly and professionally in a closed loop environment. There are many considerations in making an RFID solution work properly which can increase the costs by multiple factors—a fact that has caught a lot of people out. A proper cost analysis must be performed and the numbers have got to stack up before any decision to deploy RFID should be taken.

Given that bar coding still hasn't been fully deployed after 40 years in the supply chain, I find it hard to accept that this much more expensive, infinitely more complicated and not yet mature technology is going to be any different. Given the last 15 years of what is effectively an RFID failure in the supply chain, insist in seeing a proven working solution before taking what is ultimately a big leap of faith. History is littered with large technical blunders—RFID in the supply chain could be one of the biggest.

Organizations to Contact

American Civil Liberties Union (ACLU)
125 Broad Street, 18th Floor, New York, NY 10004
(212) 549-2500
Web site: www.aclu.org

Founded in 1920, the ACLU is a nonprofit and nonpartisan organization that focuses on basic freedoms, such as the right to privacy. It has more than 500,000 members and supporters and handles nearly 6,000 court cases annually from offices in almost every state. The ACLU's Technology and Liberty Project monitors civil liberties issues arising from emerging technology.

Association for Automatic Identification and Mobility (AIM Global)
AIM Global, Warrendale, PA 15086
(724) 934-4470 • fax: (724) 934-4495
e-mail: info@aimglobal.org
Web site: www.aimglobal.org

AIM Global is the international trade association for technologies that identify, track, record, store, and communicate data, including radio-frequency identification (RFID) and bar codes. Its RFID Experts Group promotes effective implementation of RFID technology.

Consumers Against Supermarket Privacy Invasion and Numbering (CASPIAN)
Web site: www.nocards.org

CASPIAN is a consumer group aimed against supermarket loyalty or frequent-shopper cards, with members across the nation and thirty countries worldwide. The group works to educate consumers, condemn marketing strategies that invade shoppers' privacy, and encourage privacy-conscious shopping habits.

Electronic Frontier Foundation (EFF)

454 Shotwell Street, San Francisco, CA   94110-1914
(415) 436-9333 • fax: (415) 436-9993
e-mail: information@eff.org
Web site: www.eff.org

EFF is an organization of students and other individuals who want to promote a better understanding of telecommunications issues. It fosters awareness of civil liberties issues arising from advancements in computer-based communications media and supports litigation to preserve, protect, and extend First Amendment rights in computing and telecommunications technologies. EFF's publications include *Building the Open Road, Crime and Puzzlement*, the quarterly newsletter *Networks and Policy*, the biweekly electronic newsletter *EFFector*, and others.

Electronic Privacy Information Center (EPIC)

1718 Connecticut Avenue, NW, Suite 200
Washington, DC   20009
(202) 483-1140 • fax: (202) 483-1248
Web site: http://epic.org

EPIC is a public interest research center in Washington, DC. It was established in 1994 to focus public attention on emerging civil liberties issues and to protect privacy, the First Amendment, and constitutional values. EPIC publishes an electronic newsletter on civil liberties in the information age—the *EPIC Alert*. It also publishes reports and books about privacy, open government, free speech, and other similar topics.

IEEE

3 Park Avenue, 17th Floor, New York, NY   10016-5997
(212) 419-7900 • fax: (212) 752-4929
Web site: www.ieee.org

Formed in the 1963 merger of the American Institute of Electrical Engineers and the Institute of Radio Engineers, IEEE is an organization of engineers, scientists, and allied professionals whose technical interests are rooted in electrical and computer sciences, engineering, and related disciplines. Its membership exceeds 365,000 and spans 150 countries. IEEE publishes many books, standards, and periodicals, including the monthly magazine, *IEEE Spectrum.*

Institute for the Future (IFTF)
124 University Avenue, 2nd Floor, Palo Alto, CA   94301
(650) 854-6322 • fax: (650) 854-7850
e-mail: info@iftf.org
Web site: www.iftf.org

IFTF is an independent nonprofit research group that specializes in technological, business, and social trends. It is based in northern California's Silicon Valley and was founded in 1968 by a group of former RAND Corporation researchers with a grant from the Ford Foundation.

Privacy Rights Clearinghouse
3100 5th Avenue, Suite B, San Diego, CA   92103
(619) 298-3396 • fax: (619) 298-5681
Web site: www.privacyrights.org

The Privacy Rights Clearinghouse is a nonprofit organization providing information and advocacy for consumers. It is primarily supported by grants and serves individuals nationwide. The organization provides extensive fact sheets on privacy issues and operates a hotline for consumers to report privacy abuses.

Bibliography

Books

Katherine Albrecht and Liz McIntyre	*The Spychips Threat: Why Christians Should Resist RFID and Electronic Surveillance.* Nashville, TN: Nelson Current, 2006.
Jerry Banks, David Hanny, Manuel A. Pachano, and Les G. Thompson	*RFID Applied.* Hoboken, NJ: Wiley, 2007.
Collin J. Bennett and David Lyon	*Playing the Identity Card: Surveillance, Security, and Identification in Global Perspective.* New York: Routledge, 2008.
Daniel M. Dobkin	*The RF in RFID: Passive UHF RFID in Practice.* Boston: Elsevier/Newnes, 2008.
Simson Garfinkel and Beth Rosenberg, Eds.	*RFID: Applications, Security, and Privacy.* Upper Saddle River, NJ: Addison-Wesley, 2006.
Bill Glover and Himanshu Bhatt	*RFID Essentials.* Sebastopol, CA: O'Reilly, 2006.
George Roussos	*Ubiquitous and Pervasive Commerce: New Frontiers for Electronic Business.* London: Springer, 2006.

Periodicals

Anna Bahney	"High Tech, Under the Skin," *New York Times*, February 2, 2006.
Sunil Chopra and Manmohan S. Sodhi	"In Search of RFID's Sweet Spot," *Wall Street Journal*, March 3, 2007.
David Coursey	"Medical RFID Tagging Could Save Lives," *eWeek*, October 15, 2004.
Mark David	"Identity Theft: RFID Muscles into Consumer Market," *Electronic Design*, February 15, 2007.
Economist	"Radio Silence," June 15, 2007.
Michael Gardner	"State Looks at Limiting Scanning Technology," *San Diego Union-Tribune*, August 19, 2007.
Terry Gardner	"RFID: A Technology to Help Bring Your Bag Home," *Los Angeles Times*, October 14, 2007.
Amal Graafstra	"Hands On," *IEEE Spectrum*, March 2007.
William Norman Grigg	"Terrorists Chip In," *American Conservative*, February 12, 2007.
Jonathan Krim	"Embedding Their Hopes in RFID," *Washington Post*, June 23, 2004.
Bill Mongelluzzo	"RFID's Big Bang: Use of the Technology Has Grown Since Wal-Mart's Directive," *Journal of Commerce*, November, 7, 2005.

Siobhan
Morrissey

"Are Microchip Tags Safe?" *Time*,
October 18, 2007.

Roy Want

"The Magic of RFID," *ACM Queue*,
October 2004.

Alec Wilkinson

"Taggers," *New Yorker*, March 20,
2006.

Lorrie Willey

"RFID and Consumer Privacy: Let
the Buyer Beware!" *Journal of Legal,
Ethical, and Regulatory Issues*, July
2007.

Index

privacy/security issues, 9, 26–27, 80–81
during removal, 7
Human tracking limitations, 40
Hutchison Port Holdings, 12
Hyan Microelectronics Co. Ltd., 13

I

IDTechEx (market analysis firm), 19
Immigration uses, 86
Industry uses
accountability, 37, 42
automotive, 103
closed system proponents, 46–47
cost concerns of, 97
by dot coms, 101
for music, 29
privacy protection by, 42–47
See also Manufacturing industry; Medical industry uses; Pharmaceutical industry uses; Retail industry uses
Informed consent, 81
International Civil Aviation Organization (ICAO), 65–66, 67, 70–71, 75–76
Internet uses
database access, 40
encryption concerns, 24
safety/security with, 15, 18, 56
Inventory tracking
for cost management, 29
by libraries, 21, 46

by manufacturing industry, 19, 95–96, 97
by retailers, 10, 19, 34, 95, 97–98
Item-level tagging, 35, 38, 47, 49, 55

J

Jaeger, Jan, 83–93
Johns Hopkins University computer lab, 24–25
Johnson, Keith, 8
Juels, Ari, 20–21, 24–25, 48–56, 92
Junkbusters (privacy rights organization), 33–47

K

Kefauver, Barry, 67–68, 71
Killing tags, 42–44, 49–50
Kronegger, Peter, 70

L

Legacy infrastructure issue, 56
Legislation/laws
for human implants, 92–93
for passports, 66
privacy rights and, 44, 53, 56
Libramation (tag manufacturer), 21–22
Limitations of RFID
capacity, 29, 78
data collection, 37
legislation, 92
myths of, 39–41
See also Cost concerns
Lockheed Martin, 12

Random Unique Identifier
(RUID), 61–62
Read-range distances
in cloners, 26–27
in contactless chips, 70
in passive tags, 13, 20
in read-write chips, 31
for retail goods, 10, 43, 46
technology impact on, 95
variances in, 34, 38, 39–40, 78,
100, 103
in VeriChip, 85, 91
Retail industry uses
for active tags, 13–14
convenience issues, 21
inventory tracking, 10, 19, 34,
95, 97–98
for manufacturing, 22, 29,
31–32
privacy protection and, 55–56
read-range distances and, 10,
43, 46
RFDump (software program), 23
Rights/responsibilities framework,
36–37
Roberti, Mark, 9
RSA Security, Inc., 32, 92

S

Sade, Robert M., 77–82
Satellite tracking of chips, 41
Savi Group, 12–13
Schneier, Bruce, 71
Security safeguards
government measures, 19, 29,
65, 68–69
Internet safety, 15, 18, 56
vs. RFID convenience, 68–70
third-party verification of, 37
See also Electronic passports;
Human implants

Seelig, Richard, 89
Sensor-based technology, 15, 18,
95, 98–99
SHA-1 encryption tool, 24–25
Silverman, Scott, 86, 87
Skimming technology, 25, 60–61,
65, 70
SmartCard technology, 14, 18, 23,
26
SpeedPass tokens, 23–24, 55
*Spy Chips: How Major Corpora-
tions and Government Plan to
Track Your Every Move*
(Albrecht), 8
State Department reviews, 57–63
Supply chain benefits
business interests *vs.* individual rights, 34
exaggerated, 100–107
global management, 12–14, 41
rights and responsibilities,
36–37, 38
significance of, 9, 94–99
Symbol Technologies (Motorola),
15

T

Tagsys (RFID maker), 21
Terrorist threats, 65–67, 68, 76, 88
Texas Instruments (TI), 19, 24–25
Toxic substance detection, 38
Tracking in store, privacy protection, 42–43
Tracking uses
bar codes and, 31, 101–102,
106–107
in closed systems, 46
for guest workers, 86–87